Practical Psychiatry: How to Use It in Daily Living

Jean Rosenbaum, M.D.

Parker Publishing Company, Inc.
West Nyack, N.Y.

© 1971, *by*

PARKER PUBLISHING COMPANY, INC.

West Nyack, N.Y.

Library of Congress
Catalog Card Number: 70-159749

ISBN-0-13-693580-X
B & P

To all those readers wise enough to seek help. This is half the battle won.

What This Book Can Do for You

This book, based on my experience as a practicing psychiatrist, can show you how to get rid of that nagging feeling of unhappiness in your life and replace it with the warm glow that comes from having a happy and successful life. It will show you how to eliminate that feeling of discontent that dogs your footsteps and drags you down; how you can have good emotional health, improved mental efficiency and a new, better, and more satisfying life!

You will not only feel better but you will also look better. You will be able to project your feelings of happiness and contentment, and when you do that you will have better relationships with others—your family, your friends, and those with whom you work. Success will become natural for you when you have learned to apply the principles of good emotional and mental health which I have explained in easy-to-understand terms in this book.

No matter who you are, what you are, or how much education you have, this book is for you and for your benefit in your daily living. It will teach you the secrets of building a better personality, how to develop the emotional health and mental poise you need in order to achieve your maximum happiness and success.

Wouldn't you like to have other people look up to you and admire you because you have such an attractive personality? Wouldn't you like to be the kind of person who can handle easily the problems of daily living that come to all of us? My book will show you how you can develop just such a desired personality.

And when you have applied the programs in this book you will not be the same person you were, subject to all kinds of worries and emotional problems. You will have learned how to take care of those problems quickly and effectively.

It doesn't matter how worried you have been, or how much tension and anxiety or frustration have crippled your life in the past. *Practical Psychiatry: How to Use It in Daily Living* will give you the key to that new, happy life you want for yourself.

This is a practical book for you if you want to help yourself to better emotional health. It will show you how you can test yourself for hidden emotional problems. It will teach you how to use self-analysis to help you reach your goal of better emotional health.

By making a self-image profile as shown in this book, you can choose the self you've always wanted to be. In only seven steps, you can remake yourself into a new personality, a dynamic and successful personality.

Crises in daily living will no longer have the power to terrorize you. The practical psychiatric techniques in this book will make it possible for you to cope with the stresses and strains of modern life.

The simple programs and tests set out here have all been tested in my professional practice. When you apply yourself conscientiously to them, they can make that vital difference in your life between happiness and unhappiness, between success and failure.

Never before has such an opportunity for applying the principles of *psychiatric* knowledge to everyday situations and problems been made available in a single volume for home use.

This is an exciting book because it can make your life exciting. It can change your life for happiness whether you are an executive, a student, a housewife, a professional person, or an individual who is on the way up the ladder of success. Whatever you do, you can do it better with the practical guidance in this book—and get more out of your life.

Good health is number one on everyone's list and so is success in life. Both of these satisfactions can be yours when you learn how to control your emotions. Both can result when you learn how to understand yourself and how to make the required changes in your personality.

You will notice beneficial changes in your daily life taking place as soon as you start to read this book and follow the programs outlined in the various chapters. It is like having a personal counselor and professional psychiatrist at your side 24 hours a day for immediate guidance in meeting any problem of daily living that confronts you.

Start today to take that first step toward better health, more success and greater happiness by using *Practical Psychiatry* as your personal guide through the complicated maze of modern daily living.

Following is a sample listing of specific aids in this book that you can use to help yourself with practical psychiatry in solving your problems of daily living:

How to make a realistic appraisal of yourself *(Chapter 1; Page 27)*.

Four requirements for happiness *(Chapter 1; Page 29)*.

Your check list for happiness *(Chapter 1; Page 33)*.

How to detect danger signs of impending emotional problems *(Chapter 2; Page 37)*.

How to handle your psychosomatic ills *(Chapter 2; Page 49)*.

How to get acquainted with your self-image *(Chapter 3; Page 54)*.

How to create a self *(Chapter 3; Page 58)*.

How to remake your personality *(Chapter 3; Page 64)*.

How to look at yourself honestly *(Chapter 4; Page 72)*.

How to understand your dreams *(Chapter 4; Page 74)*.

Writing a self-analysis *(Chapter 4; Page 74)*.

How to determine whether or not you are in the right job *(Chapter 5; Page 84)*.

How to get the most out of your job *(Chapter 5; Page 93)*.

How to get more out of your leisure *(Chapter 6; Page 102)*.

Ways in which to spend your leisure time *(Chapter 6; Page 105)*.

How to understand criticism *(Chapter 7; Page 109)*.

How to build up self-esteem *(Chapter 7; Page 115)*.

How to use criticism *(Chapter 7; Page 119)*.

How to get along with the opposite sex *(Chapter 8; Page 131)*.

How to develop an acceptable sexual profile *(Chapter 9; Page 147)*.

The six fundamental needs of marriage *(Chapter 10; Page 151)*.

How your emotional response determines the success and happiness of your marriage *(Chapter 10; Page 154)*.

A transference test for marriage *(Chapter 10; Page 156)*.

How to test your emotional responses to your marriage *(Chapter 10; Page 157)*.

How to test the family conflict level *(Chapter 11; Page 165)*.

Using family therapy to solve family problems *(Chapter 11; Page 173)*.

How to investigate the causes of your accident or illness *(Chapter 12; Page 181)*.

How to change your accident-prone personality *(Chapter 12; Page 186)*.

How to adjust to unavoidable illnesses or accidents *(Chapter 12; Page 188)*.

How to be friends with yourself *(Chapter 13; Page 194)*.

Handling your loneliness *(Chapter 13; Page 196)*.

How to recognize neurotic symptoms in others *(Chapter 14; Page 210)*.

How you should respond to a neurotic individual *(Chapter 14; Page 218)*.

How you can help your neurotic family member *(Chapter 14; Page 220)*.

Jean B. Rosenbaum

Contents

Current Living in Our Marriage-Oriented Modern Culture • The
Dilemma of the Single Person • The Danger of Accepting the
Single-Person Stereotype as Your Image • Social and Recreational
Adjustments of the Single Person • Rejection of the Opposite Sex
Can Occur in Marriage • How to Know and Remove the Causes of
an Unhappy Marriage • Sexual Identification Problems • The Sur-
rogate Principle • Rejection of the Opposite Sex Caused by Dis-
appointment in the Parent of the Opposite Sex • How Family
Patterns Can Build Sexual Defense Walls • How Your Physical
Attitude May Express Your Hidden Sexual Fears • Changing
Your Childhood Defenses • The Role of Competition with the
Opposite Sex • How to Overcome Over-Aggressiveness with the
Opposite Sex • How to Overcome Timidity and Fear with the
Opposite Sex • Breaking the Negative Courtship Pattern • How to
Become Psychologically Ready for the Opposite Sex • A
Reminder

Hidden Motivations in Sexual Relations • Some Questions to
Answer About Your Hidden Motivations • How Sexual Patterns
Reflect the Total Personality • How Your Sexual Attitudes Re-
flect Your Emotional Awareness • The Conflict Between Sexual
Desire and Society's Rules and How to Resolve It • The Role of
the Instincts and Their Conflict with Reality • Neurotic Illness
and Sexual Conflict • Childhood Trauma and Adult Sex Habits •
The Danger of Using Sex to Fight Loneliness • How Sexual Con-
tacts Are Used for Emotional Reassurance • Sexual Masochism of
Older Women • The Sexual Profile of the Flirtatious Woman •
The Don Juan Personality • How Homosexual Fears Can Inhibit
Your Sexual Development • How Contempt and Other Hostile
Fixations Can Influence Your Sexual Life • How to Test for
Hostility Toward Members of the Opposite Sex • How the Fear
of Sexual Frigidity or Impotence Can Be Overcome • How You
Can Develop a Socially Acceptable and Emotionally Rewarding
Sexual Profile • A Reminder

Parent Image and Adult Behavior in Accident and Illness • Sickness and Sex • How to Determine if You Are Actually Accident Prone • How to Change an Accident-Prone Personality • Understanding Psychosomatic Illnesses • How to Accept the Problems of Bona Fide Accidents and Illnesses • How to Adjust to Accidents and Illnesses in the Family Circle • Regression in Illness • How to Cope with Your Own Accident or Illness • Six Steps to Help You in Your Illness or Accident Situation • How Much Can Be Learned and How New Maturational Levels Can Be Reached as a Result of Crises • A Reminder

Living Alone in Modern Society • Be Friends with Yourself • Responses to Loneliness • Six Negative Responses to Loneliness • How to Avoid Negative Responses to Loneliness • Drugs Are Not the Answer • Hypochondria as a Substitute for Friends • How to Cope with Loneliness Caused by Death of a Spouse or Other Loved One • How to Adjust to Loneliness Caused by Personal Illness • How to Overcome Loneliness Caused by Moving to a New Place • How to Cope with the Loneliness Caused by a New Job • How to Handle Loneliness in Children • How to Avoid Loneliness When You Are Older • How You Can Change Your Childish Reactions to Mature Ones and Avoid Loneliness • How You Can Cure Your Feelings of Loneliness by Thoughts and Acts of Concern and Love Toward Others • A Reminder

What Do We Mean by a Neurotic? • How to Recognize the Symptoms of Neurotic Behavior • Check List of Neurotic Symptoms • Causes of Neurotic Behavior • Why Neurotic Symptoms Occur • How to Discover the Situational Problems That Cause Emotional Problems • Reasons for Neurotic Behavior • Five Basic Reasons for Reaction • Ambivalence as a Cause of Emotional Problems • How to Distinguish Between Neurosis and Psychosis • How You Can Receive Outside Help for the Family Member with Emotional Problems • How to Respond Toward the Neurotic • How the Past Influences the Present • How the

1

The Necessity to Develop Happiness

as a Basis for Richer Living

Happiness is the big ingredient everyone wants in his life. Not everybody agrees on what it is; and not everybody agrees on how to develop it. Happiness is, in many ways, a personal matter. There are paths you can take to develop your individual happiness. In this chapter I am going to point out to you these paths—paths *you* can follow.

There are three things to remember about happiness:

1. Happiness is important.
2. Happiness is desirable.
3. Happiness is possible.

No matter what your past circumstances have been, no matter what your present conditions are, happiness is possible for you. You can learn to develop it. This happiness will give you a healthier and richer life.

THE EGO

One of the psychological terms which you will meet frequently in these pages is the term *ego.* The ego is a psychological division of the brain, not an anatomical part.

Let us think of the mind as divided into three parts, the *ego,* the *id* and the *superego.* The *id* contains the instinctual and aggressive drives such as anger, sexual drives and repressed memories. The *superego* contains the ego ideal and guilt systems. Most of the id and the superego are part of your *unconscious*. They will be discussed in more detail in later chapters of this book.

The *ego* is the most accessible part. It is primarily conscious, or easily made conscious. We have storehouses of memories, of knowledge which we can bring out into the open. These belong in the area we call the *preconscious*.

The ego itself most nearly matches what you think of yourself. It is your own mirror reflection of your personality. *"This is me,"* is what you exclaim when you look at your ego.

The ego is the mediator between the external demands of reality, your external environment, and the internal demands of the id. It makes the necessary compromises between your internal sexual and aggressive demands and the outside world.

Picture the id as the pleasure and destruction seeking region of the mind—irresponsible and a delinquent. The superego is the repository of our goals, ethics and morals, and acts as judge and jury. The ego is an overworked attorney, dealing with the demands of the id, the pressures of the superego, and the realities of the external social system.

HAPPINESS IS A BASIC EGO PROBLEM

Happiness which is many things to many people, has sometimes been called indefinable. However, happiness *can* be defined since it is an ego problem.

Happiness is a state of well-being. It is quiet joyfulness and contentment. It is experienced within the ego when all three regions of the mind—ego, id, and superego—are in balance and harmony with each other. That is when the demands of the drives are enough satisfied to give pleasure yet not overly expressed so that there is conflict with external realities. Neither are there offenses against the superego with its strict standards, its conscience, and its sense of guilt. These things, overindulgences, endanger your ego. When your ego is in danger, so are you, and then you are an unhappy person.

TOOLS OF THE EGO

The ego has a number of tools that enable it to carry out its various functions as mediator or coordinator.

1. It is in control of the muscular-skeletal system.
2. It contains all the sensory perceptions.
3. It has a large library of available memories which we call *past experiences.* Thought processes are stored in the ego.

Your relationship with your own body is an ego process. Your body image is an ego process; control of your motor abilities is within your ego; your ability to communicate with others and your own measure of understanding are all in the province of your ego.

By controlling your drives before they get out of hand, the ego helps you toward your happiness. This is the process of *neutralization,* which will be discussed in more detail under "The Connection of Emotional Maturity to Happiness" (page 32).

HAPPINESS IS AN ACHIEVEMENT WITHIN YOUR REACH

Happiness is possible for anyone. It is waiting for you! It is an achievement you can claim as your own. You are not born happy, but rather you develop your capacity for happiness. One step of happiness can lead to another step.

Happiness is not achieved by devious or false methods. The first step to building a state of happiness in your life is to raise the level of your own self-respect.

Happiness is only within your reach if you first admit that it is a definite possibility. Once you have reached that awareness, you can reorient your thinking and life-style toward happiness.

THE HANDICAPS OF FALSE IDEAS ABOUT HAPPINESS

Just as many people try to find or achieve happiness in undesirable and unrewarding ways, so many people have false, psychologically unsound ideas about happiness. Do you suffer from the handicap of such ideas?

A common false idea about happiness is the *single issue conception.* This is the idea that your happiness depends on one thing. If you are unhappy, ask yourself if you are practicing this exclusion principle in your life. By concentrating on one thing, are you overlooking other things that could bring you happiness?

Homer's Fallacies about Happiness in Business

Homer, a minor executive in a large company, thought that he could be happy only if he was in business for himself. He felt miserable and he made his family miserable.

"Until you can get your own business, why not enjoy what you are doing?" suggested a friend.

Homer was indignant at this remark. He quickly pointed out that he could be happy only when he was free from his company duties and responsibilities. He had closed his eyes and mind to all other possibilities of happiness in his life. He was not only putting all of his eggs into one basket—he was literally concentrating on one egg!

For financial and other reasons, Homer was not able to go into his own business. Since he could not reconcile his dream of happiness with the realities of his life, he doomed himself and his family to a life of frustration and unhappiness. But there *were* things he could have done.

His friend's advice was sound. Homer should have listened to him. He should have been willing to accept the facts of his life as they were. The work he was doing, while not his first choice, was a potential source of enjoyment. He could have explored the possibilities of starting his own business on a part-time basis. If this was not practical, he could have begun to plan on paper his future business life.

Homer only complained. He did not take any forward steps. By refusing to take any positive action, Homer guaranteed his own unhappiness.

YOU DON'T HAVE TO BE HAPPY ALL DAY FOR NORMAL HAPPINESS

Another frequent misconception about happiness is the idea

that it should be a continual state of being. This is an unrealistic idea. You may be happy for several hours in each day or for a period of time. It need not be consecutive segments of time.

Not being happy does not mean being unhappy in the ordinary sense of the word. No one should expect to live in a constant state of extreme elation or euphoria.

An intense preoccupation or worry about your happiness should alert you that something is wrong. It is as absurd and abnormal to be continually checking the intensity of your happiness as it would be to take your body temperature at hourly intervals when there is no illness that requires it.

A reasonable goal is to be happy for several hours each day.

HAPPINESS IS NOT JUST FOR THE YOUNG

Some people think that happiness is the special province of the young. You may have heard some of your friends lamenting the passing of the so-called "carefree years." Perhaps you yourself look back with a certain amount of longing at your earlier years, years you remember as being less complicated and happier.

This is false. It is illogical reasoning and poor remembering. A *realistic* appraisal of youthful years will show that they were more often times of tenseness, anxiety, and general unhappiness. This is the period when adolescents are struggling to express themselves and develop their personalities. At the same time, they are being forced to compete in the adult world.

Therefore, one of your first steps toward achieving happiness is to rid yourself of these psychologically false ideas about happiness.

IS HAPPINESS DEPENDENT UPON SENSUAL GRATIFICATION?

The sensory perceptions in your life are one of the functions of the ego. These are powerful factors in your life.

Gratification is an act or thought which takes away tension and relieves anxiety. It gives you pleasure, either actual or anticipatory.

Sensual gratification is a necessary part of your happiness pattern. These are the pleasures obtained through your sensory organs. *Taste, touch, smell, sight,* and *sound* all contribute to your sense of well-being. When they are in balance and are used, you are getting more out of life. You are happier.

You *need* this sensual gratification in your life. But moderation is necessary. There is no happiness in the misuse of sensual gratification. As in the case of anything which is overdone, the end results are pain, not pleasure. Misuse means unhappiness rather than happiness.

Ask yourself—in what areas of my life do I need to improve my sensual gratifications? Am I hurrying through my meals too fast? How long has it been since I last listened to a piece of music? Slow down if necessary and take time out for *looking, smelling, tasting, touching, and hearing.* Look at that sunset, listen to that bird, touch the bark of a tree or feel that rock you've just picked up. Smell how the air reflects the weather, the time of day.

Too many people fail to strike the proper balance in sensual gratification. You can, if you are willing to adjust your life patterns to accommodate the right amount of sensory awareness. Much of your happiness is literally at your fingertips. It is within your hearing and sight. It is waiting to be tasted and smelled. *Sensual gratification is not to be avoided but to be enjoyed.*

How Mary Lou A. Found Her Happiness

"Supreme happiness consists in self-content," wrote Jean Jacques Rousseau, the French philosopher and reformer.

I thought of that when Mary Lou A., a widow, came to me for help. She looked unhappy. Her face was creased with frown lines, making her look much older than her 53 years. Her voice bordered on a whine.

"I'm not happy any more, Doctor," she complained. "I feel so discontented with my life."

"When were you happy?" I asked her.

Her face softened as she thought back to the past, and she said that she had been the happiest when her husband was alive and her children were at home. At that time she had been kept busy cooking big meals, sewing, and doing all of the hundreds of things you need to do when you keep house for a family.

Mary Lou's happiness was directly connected to her feelings of usefulness. At the time she came to see me, she admitted that she didn't really know where her time went. She watched television, went to movies, played bridge occasionally, and visited friends and relatives.

Actually, it was a remark about one of her relatives that solved Mary Lou's problem and brought her happiness again. In talking about her relatives, she mentioned a cousin of hers. This cousin, only slightly older than she, had become severely handicapped because of an accident.

"Could you be of some help to your cousin?" I asked.

She confessed that she had never thought of it. She liked her cousin and enjoyed visiting with her because, despite her handicap, she was cheerful and interested in the world. I advised Mary Lou to see how she could help her cousin and incidentally herself.

Mary Lou *did* find happiness and contentment again when she was once more doing something useful and meaningful with her life.

HAPPINESS IS KNOWING YOUR TRUE IDENTITY

It is important to know your true identity, for you will not be happy if you fail to see yourself in a true perspective. Part of happiness consists of knowing and fulfilling your internal capacities, which requires a realistic appraisal of what you are capable of doing.

Ask yourself:

1. What am I?
2. What am I capable of?
3. Am I attempting to deceive myself?
4. Am I being realistic?

Try this five-part exercise in self-appraisal:

1. Write down your desired goals.
2. Write down an honest appraisal of your capabilities and qualifications to achieve those goals.
3. Study the two lists.
4. Do they go well together?
5. Do they make sense?

If you get negative answers to 4 and 5, you have two choices. The first is to *increase your abilities* to make your goals attainable. This can be done through study and work, but this solution is not always possible or wise. The second choice is to *change your goals.*

Happiness is having goals which are suitable for you—and reasonably possible as well.

How Andrew J. Changed His Goal

Andrew J., a patient I once treated, was a man who at the age of 51 had decided that he wanted to be a major league baseball player. This was unrealistic not only in view of his age, but also in terms of his physical condition.

Gradually he learned to change this drive into a more realistic one—that of helping a Little League baseball team. He found his happiness in helping boys develop into ball players and watching them become proficient in the sport he loved.

HOW CHILDHOOD MENTAL INJURIES AFFECT
ADULT HAPPINESS

The shadows of childhood fears and incidents are cast over adulthood. Often some rigidly repressed childhood experience is the basis of adult fear and unhappiness. Through analysis these experiences can be brought to the surface and seen in their proper perspective. Once having gained an insight into the original mental injury or trauma, it is possible to resolve it.

How Helen R. Discovered the Key to Her Happiness

Whenever I think of a person who has been successful in discovering the key to happiness in adulthood, I think of Helen R. Helen had come from a broken home. Her own marriage had ended badly. She had nothing but unhappiness in her life.

"I looked in the mirror one day," Helen told me, "and I could see the image of the embittered and unhappy woman I was becoming. I decided then and there to see what I could do to change that image."

Analysis revealed that much of Helen's trouble came from her childhood. The many quarrels she had been forced to witness between her parents had left her with a bitter attitude toward people and particularly toward marriage. She had to learn to eliminate these feelings.

Helen went into practical nurse training. She went to work in a hospital, where she found her happiness in serving others. But greater happiness was in store for Helen for later she met a man with whom she made a happy and successful marriage.

HOW TO PREPARE YOURSELF TO EXPECT AND RECEIVE HAPPINESS

You need to prepare yourself for happiness just as you would prepare for any possible occurrence. *Happiness breeds happiness.* You need to start by being ready to accept it.

Perhaps you know people who say,"I would like to be happy but I can't!" Do you ever say that about yourself?

How can you prepare yourself? One way is to *take down your barriers* against happiness. You may have unconsciously adopted a defensive attitude toward happiness. These attitudes are caused by earlier experiences of rejection by a loved one, a friend, or by an important person. The child who rushes home to share a school triumph with his mother and is greeted only with indifference will more than likely grow up to be afraid of happiness. He will not expect to have it in his life.

If you resist happiness, it may be because you are afraid. You may be afraid to share your life and feelings with others. You must learn that your personality will only be enhanced and grow when you can share. The fear of personality diminishment is indicative of the emotionally immature person.

You must be *receptive to happiness*. You should not say, as some people do, that happiness does not exist, that happiness is a myth. Happiness does exist, and it is within your reach. You have been hurt in the past by either indifference or rejection, but you *do not* need to continue to expect to receive these negative responses.

Start each day by expecting to find happiness. As you continue reading this chapter, you will find practical suggestions on how you can achieve personal happiness.

FOUR REQUIREMENTS IN A PROGRAM FOR HAPPINESS

Happiness is possible, but it does require that you do something yourself. You need only follow these simple and reasonable rules in your pursuit of happiness:

1. *Take an interest in the world around you.* You are living in the wider world that includes *all* of humanity. You must accept the fact that you are a part of that world, that humanity. Your interest in the world should naturally extend to a desire to help and share in the work of the world, which leads to the next rule.

2. *Have a willingness to work intensely.* Work means an involvement with other people; it means extending the limits of your personal interests. It is to be, as John Donne put it, "involved in mankind." It means not just doing the daily job which you must do to earn your living, but doing something *special* with that job. That extra effort and added interest can bring you dividends of happiness.

3. *Have an appreciation of leisure.* Leisure means freedom from the demands and responsibilities of work or duty. It does *not* mean the absolute cessation of all effort.

Leisure is a psychological necessity in our complex, busy lives. It is also an opportunity for you to exchange your routine patterns for new and stimulating experiences. It is not necessary to go far afield for these experiences nor does it require a great outlay of money. The individual who sighs and complains that he can find nothing to do in his spare time is suffering from an emotional blindness. He is cheating himself out of a part of his life.

This subject of your leisure and how to use it for your best mental health is so important that I have devoted an entire chapter to the subject. At this point, it is sufficient to say that *leisure is the source of your energy renewal* and an important factor in determining your happiness.

4. *Have an understanding of solitude.* There are times when we must be alone, and times when we should be alone, but being alone often produces panic in the emotionally maladjusted.

Ask yourself these questions about solitude.

1. How do you feel about being alone?
2. Does it frighten you?
3. Do you feel uncomfortable with yourself?
4. Do you try to avoid periods of solitude?

If you answer *yes* to the last three questions above, then you should try to discover why you feel about solitude as you do. You should look forward to your periods of solitude. Being alone gives you a chance to sit down with yourself and assess your situation honestly. If you can't face this situation, you need to make whatever changes are necessary so that you can get maximum value from your periods of solitude.

Throughout this book, there will be suggestions on how you can use self-analysis and other approved psychiatric aids to free your personality from inhibiting emotional disorders. Eventually you will find that you look forward to your periods of solitude. Creative solitude can be used to meet and solve your problems. It can also be used as a fertile field in which new ideas can take root and grow.

Learn to live with yourself and your quiet moments. It will increase your happiness. *You can do it if you try.*

How an Active Interest in the World Helped George M. Build a Happy Life

I always have a special feeling of pride and happiness when I think of George M. Most people who know or meet George share this same feeling.

At first glance, you might wonder why George has such a happy personality, considering his circumstances. George has multiple sclerosis, which has confined him to a wheelchair for 15 years. He has limited use of his hands. Yet George has made a successful and happy personality adjustment to his disabling disease.

"At first I was very despondent," George admitted, "but then I decided I wasn't going to give up on the world even if it looked as if the world had given up on me!"

George took a correspondence course in salesmanship. "I liked to talk to people," he explained, "so I decided I would be a good salesman. I knew my first big job would be in selling myself. It wasn't easy but I did succeed."

At first George worked as a telephone solicitor for a local advertising firm. Now he makes radio advertisements for the same company. He writes his own copy, using a typewriter.

"I'm slow, but accurate," he says with a grin. "I really look forward to each day."

Yes, George M. is leading a useful and happy life. He doesn't deny the fact of his handicap but he hasn't let it keep him from his happiness.

THE CONNECTION OF EMOTIONAL MATURITY TO HAPPINESS

Emotional maturity is essential for happiness. It is part of the process of acceptance—acceptance of ourselves.

You can have emotional maturity, the lack of which may be keeping you from your happiness. You can exchange your frustrations, anxieties, and fears for happiness through the process of emotional maturation.

One form of this maturation is *neutralization*, a function of the ego. The ego checks the drives of the id before they get out of hand. This checking is done by neutralizing the drives. The ego takes the drives and robs them of their destructive energy, transferring that energy into creative work or play impulses. The less the drives from the id are in conflict with the ego and superego, the more energy is available for work and play.

Much of your happiness depends upon your ability to neutralize these direct drives from the id. This is the way it works: John Smith has a bad day at work. He feels like killing the boss. Instead he comes home and mows the lawn or plays a fast game of tennis. He *transfers* that energy into something socially and emotionally acceptable.

Life is a continual series of conflict situations. The way in which you respond to those situations determines your happiness.

SEVEN CHARACTERISTICS OF HAPPY PEOPLE

You can identify happy people, for they have certain common characteristics. They often seem to have an extra dimension to their personalities; they are individuals who are using their abilities to the fullest capacity; they have emotionally and psychologically integrated personalities.

I have observed many people and found that there are seven principal characteristics of happy people, as follows:

1. *Happy people are thinking people.* They are ingenious and inventive. They have learned how to be creative. They face life

realistically and are aware of both its pleasures and its pitfalls. They are able to understand and to accept a true picture of their lives.

2. *Happy people are considerate people.* Consideration for others does make you happy. It makes you feel good. Others will respond to you with consideration, and life will seem easier and pleasanter.

3. *Happy people have better health.* Their physical health is at a high level and reflects their level of emotional health. The happy person is enjoying life. He hasn't time for sickness. You may have physical handicaps, or suffer from the effects of a chronic disease or disabling accident. But if you are a happy person, you will be able to have a successful and happy life *despite* your physical limitations. You have read this story in the case of George M., and I am sure that you could furnish other examples from your own experience.

4. *Happy people show their age less.* Happy people actually seem to age at a slower rate. They often have better posture and better color. They are more alert than some of their contemporaries who are suffering from depression and anxiety.

5. *Happy people like themselves.* Self-respect is essential to happiness. You have to live with yourself, and you aren't going to be happy living with someone you don't like or respect.

6. *Happy people are liked by others.* Do you remember the old saying: "Laugh and the world laughs with you; cry, and you cry alone"? This is true. We are naturally drawn toward happy people just as we naturally try to avoid being with unhappy people

7. *Happy people are successful in what they do.* They are always willing to invest their time in trying new experiences. Their success is measured in terms of enrichment, enlightenment, and personal satisfaction.

YOUR PERSONAL CHECK LIST MAKING HAPPINESS POSSIBLE FOR YOURSELF

Here are some very practical helps for you in your quest for happiness. These are suggestions based on my experience as a practicing psychiatrist.

There are six things which you can do to grow or <u>increase</u> <u>happiness</u>. They are not elaborate; they require nothing but your cooperation. If you have confidence in them, *they will work for you.* Here they are:

1. Add up your <u>blessings</u> and catalog them. You may have more than you think. Take a piece of paper and write them down. These blessings may be readily apparent to you; they may be spiritual or emotional in nature. If you are like most people, your list of blessings will include some of all of these.

2. List your <u>past accomplishments</u> and achievements. Do not eliminate any but list everything which, no matter how small, was in the nature of a personal triumph. It may have been a new skill which you learned or it may have been an improvement in an old one. Perhaps it was completing a difficult task. Often it will not have been a public triumph at all, but a private one. You can and should take pride in your previous accomplishments. Knowing them will help you to build your self-esteem, and a high level of self-esteem is needed for happiness.

3. List your <u>anticipations</u> that you feel are attainable. Anticipation can play a big part in your happiness. Looking forward and planning are attributes of the happy person. *We all have something to anticipate.* It may be a vacation, a pleasant evening with friends, attendance at a concert, or a ball game.

4. Learn how to sharpen and develop your powers of <u>observation</u>. Part of developing happiness is to sharpen and develop your powers of observation. Don't go through life as if you had no senses. Life is to be *seen, felt, tasted, smelled,* and *heard.* You have the capacity to do all of those things. You might try keeping a notebook in which you record your observations. You will find that as your perception increases, so does your happiness.

5. Learn how to take time to <u>enjoy</u> your life. Time is flexible. You can use it wisely or poorly. You can make it a part of your happiness program. Don't hurry through your life. Take time out to enjoy the world around you. Don't put off your life. Don't exist on a half-alive plane of incomplete awareness. Happiness comes from total commitment each minute to what you are doing or thinking at that particular time.

6. *Learn how to replace fear in your life with happiness.* Fear is crippling and must be replaced by confidence. Fears are common to us all, but we do not need to hang on to them. Fears and other anxieties should be carefully examined as to their origin, truth, and solution.

When you have completed steps 1 - 3 of this check list, you will find it easier to expose and handle the illogic behind your fears.

A REMINDER

Happiness is possible. It means contentment and fulfillment as an individual. It can mean professional and financial success. It does mean social and personality success. You will be happy with yourself and show that happiness to others.

Happiness starts with you. The first step is to decide that you *want* to be a happy person. Once you have made that decision, you can move toward your goal. Start working on your happiness check list. Don't sabotage your life by a lack of faith in yourself.

The seven characteristics of happy people can also be *your* characteristics.

2

How to Tell the Early Signs
of Emotional Problems

Emotional problems can occur in your life at any time. They can and do occur in nearly everybody's life at some time. Occasionally, as you will see, they are short in duration and weak in intensity. You may scarcely be aware of them. At other times, however, an emotional problem may cause you considerable mental and physical distress.

Emotional problems are *not* mental illnesses. If unchecked they might lead to more serious mental trouble. Just as a stomach ache does not necessarily mean cancer, an emotional problem does not necessarily mean a mental breakdown.

A continual emotional problem, like a persistent stomach ache, will make you uncomfortable. It will impair your ability to function as a well-integrated personality.

In this chapter I am going to show you how to cope with your periods of emotional stress. You can help yourself achieve and keep your emotional health balance.

EMOTIONAL PROBLEMS DON'T ALWAYS JUST HAPPEN OVERNIGHT

Emotional problems have a starting point. They may be produced by a shock, an incident, a personality flaw or weakness, or by twisted and inappropriate reactions to other people and events. When you discover the origin of your emotional problem then you have started on your way to learning how to handle it.

Sudden shocks can cause an immediate emotional reaction which turns into an emotional problem. A common such shock is the death of a family member or friend. Even the death of a well-known public figure can be the cause of lingering emotional reactions. The way in which the death occurs accounts for much of the emotional shock. Sudden or violent death may result in serious emotional problems for the survivors. It is more usual, however, for an emotional problem to develop over a long period of time.

It is important to discover these emotional problems in their earliest stages. You can teach yourself to look for and recognize the early signs of emotional problems.

YOUR THREE-POINT PROGRAM FOR EMOTIONAL PROBLEMS

As we go on through this chapter, I would like you to keep in mind your three-point program for coping with emotional problems, as follows:

1. Recognize the early signs of emotional problems.
2. Discover the origins of your emotional problems.
3. Plan positive ways to handle these problems.

With these in mind, the following sections will help you to attack your special problems.

TEN DANGER SIGNS OF IMPENDING EMOTIONAL PROBLEMS

There are ten common, easily recognized signs of emotional problems. You can suffer from one or a combination of several of them. They all represent a deviation from normal behavior and attitudes, and mean trouble somewhere in your life pattern and personality structure.

These ten danger signs are:

1. Feelings of anxiety
2. Restlessness
3. Inability to make decisions

  4. Irritableness
  5. Feelings of sadness
  6. Insomnia
  7. Loss of appetite
  8. Emotional over-eating
  9. Fatigue
  10. Lack of interest in your work or surroundings.

Do *you* have any of these symptoms? Following is a guide for your use in recognizing these ten danger signals:

1. *Feelings of anxiety.* Anxiety is a signal of tenseness which takes place in the ego. This is a feeling of fear and uncertainty, a painful state of insecurity.

Another way of describing anxiety is to say that it is inter-psychic tension. It is a manifestation of conflict between the various compartments of the psyche or mind. For example, if there is an impulse from the id such as a sexual urge or a repressed memory, the ego defenses are activated. The conflict between the id and the ego produces tension. The conflict is buried in the mind; the tension is felt by the mind and body.

There also can be conflict between the superego and the ego. The superego, as we have learned, contains the guilt system. In other words, the superego is your "do and do not" system which you learned and incorporated from your parents.

A common modern term for anxiety is the word *uptight*. This is actually quite descriptive of the uncomfortable feeling that you have when you suffer from anxiety.

How Bernard T. Was Able to Overcome His Feelings of Anxiety

Bernard T., a successful businessman, came to me because he was suffering from feelings of anxiety which had robbed him of all his joy of living.

On the surface, Bernard would appear to have no reasons for his tense, nervous condition. He had been happily married for nearly 40 years. He had a pleasant relationship with his grown children and enjoyed his grandchildren. His business was economically sound and, in fact, had recently expanded.

It was discovered by analysis that Bernard was suffering anxiety due to a business problem that he had tried to repress. He had always prided himself on his honesty, a trait which had been strongly emphasized by his parents. Recently a new accountant had suggested and used some business practices for tax purposes which Bernard felt were ethically doubtful. The accountant had told Bernard not to worry, but his superego could not be silenced. His inter-psychic conflict caused his feelings of anxiety.

Relief from that anxiety was possible when Bernard refused to allow the accountant to continue to use those methods which were morally offensive to him.

2. *Restlessness.* Restlessness is the motor or physical expression of anxiety. It means that the anxiety has shifted from being inside the mind to outside. It has gone from the mental to the physical state.

The man or woman who can't settle down to one thing is exhibiting restless behavior. The individual who feels a compulsion to keep busy is suffering from restlessness. This person usually complains of not being able to relax. Constant talking, nervous, meaningless gestures and actions are all symptoms of restlessness. You should pay attention to any signs of restlessness that you may develop. These are signals of anxiety.

Restlessness wastes energy. You are losing part of your creative life when you succumb to and continue in a pattern of restlessness.

3. *Inability to make decisions.* The inability to make decisions is related to self-doubt. Ordinarily, we make hundreds of decisions in the course of a typical day. Most of these are automatic in nature and do not require soul-searching judgment. A small percentage of our daily decisions do involve important issues and call for more elaborate thinking processes.

An individual who finds it difficult to make a final decision is in emotional trouble. He has doubts about his own ability, and although these doubts are usually without foundation they are real enough to him to keep him from acting.

The inability to make decisions is sometimes a regressive action. By that I mean a going back to the period of childhood or adolescence. This often happens to an individual whose parents were extremely dominating.

A patient whose father had made *all* of his decisions for him, found himself unable to make important decisions after his father died.

"When a crisis occurs or a decision must be made, I am literally paralyzed mentally. I just can't seem to be able to think," he said.

He had to build up his self-confidence. Once he had convinced himself of his own worth, he was able to make his own decisions.

Closely allied with this problem of decision making and emotional problems is the inability to judge the relative importance and necessity of various decisions. It is a sign of emotional trouble if you find that you spend as much time agonizing over what to eat for lunch as you do deciding on some facet of your job or professional responsibility.

Be aware of your own worth and ability. Trust yourself to make competent judgments in those areas which are part of your knowledge.

4. *Irritableness.* Irritableness is a kind of mental restlessness. It is a peevish response to other people and situations. To the outsider there frequently seems to be no real or readily apparent reason for the state of irritability.

Do you find yourself flying off the handle easily? Are you easily upset?

If you are irritable, you can be helped. Like all the other signs of emotional problems, irritableness has an origin. Try keeping track of those things which irritate you. Are the things which supposedly irritate you, the actual causes? You may find that there are deeper causes below the surface—perhaps below your immediate consciousness.

How many of those causes can you eliminate from your life? How important are they in relation to the rest of your life?

Irritableness like restlessness uses up your energy. It also has an effect upon all of your personal relationships. The irritable personality is an unpleasant one. You do not have to display irritableness. With some effort and personal determination, you can avoid the causes of irritation. Put the emphasis in your life on the important things.

How Irritableness Was Handled in Two Cases

When the tire factory closed down, both M. A. and Mr. B. were suddenly unemployed. This was an unexpected blow to each of them for they had families to support, payments to make, and a certain standard of living to maintain.

Understandably they became depressed and anxious. Mr. A., who had previously been an even-tempered man, became very irritable, to the surprise and distress of his family. Mr. B., on the other hand, had not had for some time a good disposition. He was considered cranky and touchy by those who knew him. After Mr. B. lost his job, his irritability increased.

In time, new management reopened the tire factory and recalled the workers. Mr. A. and Mr. B. returned to their jobs. Mr. A.'s irritableness vanished. The emotional problem caused by his economic worries was solved. Mr. B. remained as cross as ever. It was not until he sought professional help that Mr. B. was able to get over his symptoms of irritableness.

The loss of the job at the tire factory, while a source of irritation to Mr. B., was not the real cause of his irritation. His irritation, the sign of his emotional trouble, was in his family relationships. Disappointed that his children would not go to college as he wanted them to, Mr. B. had developed doubts about his role as a father. His wife blamed him for the way in which the children were determined to oppose their parents.

After therapy and counseling, Mr. B. was able to see how he could better communicate with his children. He also learned to respect them as individuals. They, in turn, were more willing to listen to him in his new non-irritable state.

5. *Feelings of sadness.* Feelings of sadness are a symptom of depression or impending depression. Depression itself is a pathological state.

There are times and causes for what we might call normal sadness or grief. Any loss will cause feelings of sadness. This can be loss by death or distance of a loved one. It can be loss of a familiar object. The loss of a pet animal is a sad occasion. The loss of one's job, as in the case of Mr. A., is a natural cause of sadness. Any disappointment will result in periods of sadness.

However, sadness as a sign of emotional problems is slightly different. If sadness has no *apparent* cause, it is an early sign of emotional distress. Sadness which is out of proportion to the loss or disappointment is another sign. Prolonged sadness indicates an inability to recover normally from shocks or disappointments.

6. *Insomnia.* Insomnia is a distress signal; it is a sign of anxiety. Sometimes it is caused by depression. However, usually persons who are depressed tend to sleep more, rather than less.

Insomnia may be a temporary condition which occurs as a result of unusual excitement or worry. It may be part of a period of great anticipation. We are all familiar with the pattern of wakefulness which may precede a trip, an examination, a meeting of special importance, or a financial crisis.

"I was so excited (or worried) that I didn't sleep a wink" is a common expression. Actually, the speaker probably *did* sleep part of the time but any deviation from normal sleep patterns is regarded as insomnia.

Prolonged insomnia is of real concern. It *does* indicate that there are emotional problems.

Do you have trouble sleeping? Think back to when you first experienced these periods of wakefulness. What was the *immediate* cause of your insomnia?

Insomnia is a disturbing break in your life rhythm. Taking sleeping pills is only a "finger in the dike" solution. To *recover* from insomnia, you must look for the emotional cause. It may help you to understand the meaning of insomnia and the importance of sleep if we talk a little bit about sleep and dreams, as follows:

Sleep and Dreams

Sleep is the other side of life. It is needed to give the body physical rest and renewed vitality. It is also needed for psychic expression.

Dreams are the way in which id tensions are satisfied or relieved. During sleep, the ego is relaxed and temporarily out of control. In dreams then you can act out your repressed fantasies, hostile aggressions, and fulfill your wishes. Since reality is suspended, there are few limitations on what you can see, do, or achieve during your dreams.

Limitations, however, are still operable. The superego, that arbiter of right and wrong, is not completely relaxed. Unlike the ego, the superego continues to exert its influence on your mind. It is the superego which can cause you to wake from a violent or unpleasant dream. Awake, your ego assumes control and reassures you that it was "only a dream" and thus can not actually hurt you or change your life.

Individuals with emotional problems are frequently troubled by their dreams. In their dreams, guilt feelings, sexual fantasies, death wishes, and other repressed emotions come out. These dreams frighten the sleeper and he tries to avoid them. The only way he can avoid dreams is by not sleeping. This fear of being caught off guard during sleep may be unconscious. The individual may claim that noise keeps him awake when it is actually forbidden desires as revealed in his dreams.

Dreams are a special way of thinking at night when our defenses are down. They serve their purpose.

You *need* your sleep. You *need* your dreams. The emotionally healthy individual does *not* need to fear sleep. In the words of Keats, he will enjoy "a sleep full of sweet dreams, and health, and quiet breathing."

7. *Loss of appetite.* Loss of appetite is normal for people who are depressed. Their physiological processes are also depressed and they lose their desire to eat. Loss of appetite is another way of saying, "I am worthless. Nobody loves me, therefore I am not worth feeding."

This is a self-destructive impulse and is often an unconscious wish to die. The person is punishing himself by starving himself.

8. *Emotional over-eating.* Sometimes, though, people overeat when depressed or anxious. They try to raise their self-esteem through eating. This has its origin in infancy. When baby cries, the mother feeds it. The fat lady sitting at the soda fountain eating a hot fudge sundae is really crying, "Love me."

Overeating is an attempt to deal with your frustrations in a primitive way.

How Ralph G. Overcame His Eating Problem

Ralph G. was emaciated and haggard when he came to my office.

"I can't eat, Doctor," he said. "I'm losing my strength. I can't work. I just don't have any appetite. I've tried all kinds of pills and special foods, but nothing has helped."

Ralph's family doctor had examined and tested him for organic causes for his eating problem. When none were discovered, he suspected that Ralph's difficulty might be emotional in origin.

Analysis gradually revealed the reasons for Ralph's eating difficulties. He was unconsciously depriving himself of food because of dissatisfaction with his job.

"I've been with the company for 12 years," he explained, "and I expected to become head of my department when the former head retired. Instead, they gave the job to Joe Smith who hasn't been there as long as I have. It isn't fair!"

No, it probably *wasn't* fair, but then, much of life is unfair, and you, like Ralph, have to learn to adjust to disappointments.

Like many adult emotional responses, Ralph's had its basis in childhood experiences. As a child, Ralph had been a finicky eater. His mother attached much importance to eating. Ralph soon discovered that he could gain attention by not eating. When he ate a full meal, he was praised and rewarded. Ralph was fighting back at the company with the only weapon in his emotional arsenal - food. His attitude and subconscious plan was, "I'll show you. I won't eat until I have what I want!"

Unfortunately for Ralph, the company did not know about his plan. Fortunately Ralph was willing and able to receive help for his emotional problem. He learned to face the realities of life including the bitter moments. He was eventually able to see the real meaning behind his loss of appetite and to change his attitude toward food.

When I last saw Ralph G., he was healthy and happy looking. He no longer had the appearance of a scarecrow.

9. *Fatigue.* Fatigue is directly related to anxiety. For one thing, anxiety uses up a lot of energy. Chronic anxiety can make you more tired than any form of physical exercise. During an attack of anxiety, an individual can lose one or two pounds.

The ego may use fatigue as an excuse to avoid conflict or an unpleasant situation. If you feel constantly tired, you can take refuge in rest instead of facing the facts of your emotional problem.

10. *Lack of interest in your work or surroundings.* When you are involved in psychic conflict, all of your energy is directed inward. It is not that you have lost interest, but you no longer have the time to be interested.

You may be using as much as 90 percent of your energy in anxiety, maintaining guilt systems, feeling depressed or keeping repressions down. There is, therefore, little or no energy left to be directed outward.

HOW TO TELL WHEN YOUR BODY IS REACTING PSYCHO-SOMATICALLY (PHYSICALLY) TO YOUR EMOTIONAL PROBLEMS

Psychosomatic symptoms are the physical expression of the ten danger signs, previously set out, of emotional problems. Those signs occur in the ego in terms of feelings and thoughts. In psychosomatic symptoms we have those same feelings and thoughts being expressed *physically.*

The ego, since it controls the muscular-skeletal system and the body organs, can express conflicts through the body. It can react to fear. It can express repressed desires and wishes.

The word *psychosomatic* means involvement of the mind, *psyche,* and the body, *soma.*

Your unhappiness is often expressed through your physical symptoms. Allergies, headaches, indigestion, and other ills *may* be caused by guilt, loneliness, frustration, and similar emotional problems. If you are unhappy or dissatisfied, then you may also be reacting *psychosomatically* to your conflict situations. You may be expressing your feelings of guilt or insecurity through a socially acceptable form of ill health which is psychosomatic in origin.

Develop your self-awareness. Learn more about your own motives. Try the practice of self-analysis. Don't be afraid to question yourself.

Organic diseases can be helped by external means such as medicine, X-ray, and other forms of treatment. Psychosomatic diseases persist until the psychic (mental) cause is discovered and treated.

SEVEN COMMON PSYCHOSOMATIC SYMPTOMS

1. Headache
2. Dizziness
3. Breathing difficulties
4. Psychosomatic heart problems
5. Indigestion and stomach cramps
6. Diarrhea

7. Sudden loss of sexual function

These symptoms are set out in detail below.

1. *Headaches.* Headaches rank with the common cold for the frequency with which they attack the human body. As you can see from the advertisements, there are many popular remedies for headaches. These pills and other nostrums only offer temporary relief for the symptoms. You can not get lasting relief until you discover and remove the *cause* of your headache.

Although there are organic causes for headaches, the majority of headaches are caused by tension. They are one way of reacting to stress. Naturally, persistent headaches should be checked out with your doctor. If there is no physical basis found for your persistent headaches, you may be using them to express hostility, frustration, guilt, fear, and other anti-social and anti-personal feelings.

There is nothing unreal about a headache. It is painful and unpleasant. In severe cases it may keep you from doing your work and enjoying your leisure.

In *Iolanthe,* by Gilbert and Sullivan, appear these apt words about headaches:

> When you're lying awake with a dismal headache, and
>> Repose is tabooed by anxiety,
> I conceive you may use any language you choose
>> To indulge in, without impropriety.

"You Give Me a Headache!"

The fact that we realize that many of our headaches are psychosomatic in origin is revealed in the daily use of such expressions as "You give me a headache!" and "That job has been a real headache!"

The child is told by his mother, "Stop your whining, you're giving me a headache!" The unhappy wife says to her husband, "I couldn't fix dinner, my head aches so badly!" The man who is trying to figure out his tangled income tax gives up because of a bad headache.

All of these individuals are expressing tension and anxiety. The mother would perhaps prefer to slap her whining child, but she has prided herself on not using force as a disciplinary measure. She feels guilty because she would like to use force, and frustrated because she can't. The result is her headache.

The unhappy wife is expressing her dissatisfaction with her marriage and her husband. By her headache, she can also punish him. What she is saying in effect is, "See here, you brute, you can't expect me to get your meals and wait on you when I'm sick!"

Getting a headache over income tax is a convenient way of running away from a difficult situation. It's an acceptable excuse for postponement.

We try to fool ourselves with headaches and other psychosomatic ills.

2. *Dizziness.* People who develop dizziness which has no organic basis fear loss of self-control.

Children who have temper tantrums often grow into adults who are prone to have dizzy spells. When seized by anger or filled with anxiety, these individuals no longer lose their tempers, but become dizzy.

Repressed memories that threaten the individual, sexual frustrations or sexual impulses that threaten to overwhelm the individual can cause dizziness.

Dizziness can be so severe that the individual faints.

How Claude Overcame His Dizzy Spells

Claude had suffered the inconvenience and unpleasantness of dizzy spells for many years. When suddenly they became more frequent and more frightening, Claude's family insisted that he get medical help.

"It's getting so bad that I'm afraid to go anywhere," complained Claude. "I can't drive anymore. A couple of weeks ago I had a real bad spell. I was on a side road, fortunately, and could pull over."

Claude had been raised by strict grandparents Analysis brought to the surface one of Claude's repressed memories and traumatic childhood experiences.

"My grandfather wouldn't let me go to the movie with the other kids in the neighborhood. I remember I got angry and yelled at him. He whipped me and sent me to my room. I didn't get any supper either. I learned my lesson though. I never talked back to him again!"

Yes, Claude *had* learned his lesson. He did not lose his temper anymore, but he *did* develop dizzy spells. This dizziness continued into his adult life.

His dizzy spells were explainable in terms of the early incident, but I was concerned about why they had suddenly become so much worse. I asked him for more details about his recent dizzy spells, especially the one which had occurred in the car.

This line of questioning brought to light Claude's unhappy work situation. The increase of his dizziness coincided with the hiring of a new foreman.

"I don't get along with him at all," Claude admitted.

By changing jobs, Claude eliminated that cause of his dizzy spells. Through analysis and treatment, he learned to understand the reasons for his condition.

Claude was able to overcome dizziness. He learned not to be afraid to express dissatisfaction and irritation. Actually, when he was not continually repressing these emotions, he was not bothered by them.

"I'm enjoying life now," he said the last time I saw him. "Things don't bug me the way they did. If I don't like something, I say so and then forget about it. I haven't had a dizzy spell in weeks!"

3. Breathing difficulties. There is a similarity between the gasping and choking of a crying baby or small child, and the breathing difficulties of an older child or adult. For some people, then, breathing problems are merely a disguised way of crying.

Asthma of psychosomatic origin may develop from such breathing difficulties. The personality of the asthmatic is frequently a dependent one. He may also suffer from a fear of separation from his mother and an unacceptable attachment to her. The asthmatic in his attacks is expressing a repressed cry for his mother.

Hyperventilation or over-breathing is a common symptom of anxiety.

4. Psychosomatic heart problems. Simulated heart trouble is another common expression of tension, anxiety, or anger. Sometimes it is a case of misplaced identification. An individual who has been around or exposed to heart trouble, either real or psychosomatic in origin, will unconsciously choose heart trouble for his own special illness.

5. *Indigestion and stomach cramps.* Indigestion, stomach cramps, and constipation are all used to disguise feelings of guilt, anger, frustration, and worry. The real feelings are repressed but find their outlet in physical symptoms. The emotionally upset child may vomit; his more socially conscious adult counterpart will get stomach cramps.

6. *Diarrhea.* Diarrhea is frequently a sign of intense anxiety. It may come from repressed anger.

Psychosomatic illnesses are ways of manipulation. By holding the shield of your illness before you, you hope to avoid or control conflict.

7. *Sudden loss of sexual function.* Both men and women can suffer from the sudden loss of sexual function. Usually psychosomatic in nature, it can originate from strong feelings of guilt, anger, or fear.

In women the condition is called *vaginismus*—a contraction of the muscles of the vagina. It is a painful condition. Sexual intercourse is almost impossible. Women may also suffer from *dyspareunia,* which is intense pain during intercourse. Emotional reasons may cause *anesthesia,* or loss of sensation in the vagina or clitoris.

Impotence, complete or partial, is the usual result in the case of male loss of sexual function. Another result is premature ejaculation.

HOW TO COPE WITH YOUR PSYCHOSOMATIC ILLS

If you have an illness that is unexplainable in terms of organic medical causes, you have a psychosomatic illness. You should first be willing to accept this diagnosis and then work on living with it or, hopefully, without it.

Don't insist that your doctor is wrong if he tells you you are in good health despite your complaints of aches, sickness, or other symptoms. Don't insist on further tests and treatment. Don't change doctors, change *your* diagnosis. You may be suffering from anger—not chronic indigestion. It may be guilt instead of your gall bladder. Those headaches may signal frustration.

If you have had your physical examination and been cleared of any disease, try some self-analysis. Here is a step by step self-analysis program to follow.

1. Select a quiet spot where you can be alone.
2. Take a notebook or note paper and a pen or pencil.
3. Write down the nature of your complaint as you have diagnosed it. For example, intense headaches, persistent coughing, frequent urination, chronic indigestion, cramps, etc.
4. Write down the frequency and time when these symptoms occur. Daily? Several times a day or only weekly? Do they happen at night? On Sundays?
5. When did you first notice these symptoms?
6. Had anything unusual happened at that time?
7. What happens to you just before you have an attack?
8. Does anyone in your family or among your acquaintances have similar symptoms?

The honest answers to these questions will help you to determine the behind-the-scene reason for your psychosomatic illness. Having learned the reason, you can then work on eliminating the cause. You may have to change jobs as Claude did. You may have to put a new interest in your life. You may have to right some wrong you have committed or lose an old grudge.

Finding out the cause is only one part of your program for coping with your psychosomatic ills. The other part is to do something about changing that cause.

A Sample Self-Analysis Sheet

Let us imagine that John Smith has found his quiet place, in his case the guestroom, and has decided to try self-analysis. His answers looked like this:

COMPLAINT: Chronic heart disease. In particular, shortness of breath and palpitations.
FREQUENCY: Several times a week, almost always at night.
FIRST NOTICED: Two years ago.

UNUSUAL OCCURRENCE: My brother was killed in an accident.

BEFORE AN ATTACK: I worry about what would happen to my family if I died suddenly.

OTHER PEOPLE I KNOW WITH SIMILAR SYMPTOMS: My best friend had a heart attack four years ago.

The picture is pretty clear, isn't it? In this case, John Smith would have to change his attitude and stop worrying.

The patient on whom this case is based did successfully alter his thinking pattern. He told himself that he had provided for his family. He reminded himself that no one has control over sudden mishaps or accidents. He went that additional step beyond the initial identification with his best friend by admitting that his friend was actually leading an active life now.

John Smith might never be able to lose his habit of worrying entirely, but he could learn to control it.

HOW TO ACHIEVE AND MAINTAIN YOUR EMOTIONAL HEALTH BALANCE

Don't be afraid to look at your feelings and fantasies. Try to correlate the things which are happening on the inside with those which are going on outside. Keep your self-esteem at a high level. Develop qualities of self-awareness. See *where* and *how* your past relates to your present. Cultivate the habit and practice of self-analysis.

A REMINDER

Anxiety, tension, and other emotional problems waste energy. They make you lose time. They keep you from the proper enjoyment of your life. They keep you from creative activities.

Don't let psychosomatic illnesses cripple your effective personal development. You can change your responses and thus change your life.

3

How to Live with Yourself
and Like it

The *self* is a composite arrangement of many things. Part of this self is inherited. It comes from our parents, grandparents, and even more distant relatives. It is also formed from our own daily experiences. An important part of the self comes from the morals, standards, and ideals which we have acquired and incorporated into our own thinking. Another part comes from our aspirations and ego identifications.

In this chapter I will show you how to look at your self-image. You will discover how the self is created—how your own self was created.

The problems of living alone do exist but *they are not insurmountable!* Best of all, you can actually remake yourself into the person you have always wanted to be. *Learn how to choose your best self.*

SELF-IMAGE—WHAT IS IT?

Self-image is a unique thing. It is you. It is how you see yourself, so stop and think about yourself!

How *do* you see yourself? You see this self in two ways, as in a double mirror. You see yourself as a physical entity with distinct body characteristics. You also see yourself in a mental way. You see your hopes, dreams, and desires. You see your accomplishments.

52

This self-image is not necessarily the way in which others see you. It may not be a true picture in terms of what you really are It may not be an accurate picture in terms of what you can do.

You may be fooling yourself! You may be cheating yourself!

CONFLICT AND SELF-IMAGE

Conflict occurs when your self-image is at a wide variance from reality. This conflict makes living either with yourself or with others difficult. You may have trouble in your job or profession.

Problems of personality and social adjustment are caused by self-image conflicts. Some of these are easily recognized. The man who thinks he is Napoleon has a self-image problem. However, most self-image conflicts are not so easily seen or acknowledged. The man who is tone-deaf but insists he can sing is a harmless nuisance. His self-image is in direct conflict with reality. He will have no problems if he sings only for himself. But if he tries to join the church choir or civic choral group, then reality will conflict with his false self-image of himself as an accomplished singer.

Conflicts are caused when our self-image is too much different from the way in which others see us. There is also a possibility for conflict when our self-image and our capabilities do not match. It is natural that we should see ourselves somewhat differently than others see us. The conflict comes when we try to impose that self-image on others, and also when we deny the validity of the outsider's view of ourselves.

The closer to reality your self-image becomes, the happier you will be.

How Constance Fought Reality with a False Self-Image

Constance came to see me because she was unhappy. She didn't get along well with other people. She lived alone and didn't like it. She felt, in her words, "all on edge."

She was in her late thirties. She held a responsible job as a bookkeeper but lately she had begun to have trouble doing her work. She did not get along as well with the people in her office as she had in a firm where she had worked previously.

On the one hand, the fact that she came to me showed a desire to change and improve her life. On the other hand, Constance at first resisted my suggestions.

"Go on a diet for one thing," I told her, "and you will feel like a new person."

"I don't need to diet," was her quick reply.

Yet Constance was obviously overweight. Glancing at her I would have estimated that she weighed *at least* 30 pounds more than she should.

Talking further with Constance brought out the fact that her self-image was of a thin person. In addition, she saw herself as an interesting person who was misunderstood and unappreciated by those around her.

Constance was in emotional trouble because she was fighting reality with a false self-image. This was causing both internal and external conflicts. As an intelligent woman, she was aware that to others she appeared fat and willful. She even admitted that she had overheard herself characterized as "dull."

The continual battle between reality and her false self-image was making her nervous. It made her appear ridiculous, even stupid to other people. Naturally she didn't get along with them. Living alone was no fun either for she was beginning to be unhappy with her faulty self-image.

Constance did finally agree to follow my advice. First she had to learn some basic facts about the self. She next learned to apply these facts to her own self.

Facing reality, as I told Constance, isn't easy. But, facing reality is an *absolute must* in developing the correct self-image. How did Constance learn to do this? She followed the same suggestions I am about to give to you.

The suggestions below will help you to become the person you have always dreamed of being by matching reality with your self-image.

HOW TO TAKE AN HONEST LOOK AT YOUR SELF-IMAGE

Sitting down in front of your imaginary mirror and looking at yourself isn't too difficult in one way. What is difficult, is *taking an honest look* at your self-image.

Why is looking honestly at yourself such a difficult thing to do?

There are three main handicaps to seeing yourself as you really are:

1. A basic desire to avoid the unpleasant and painful.
2. An excessive modesty or humility.
3. An exaggerated sense of your own importance or ability.

Constance, for example, found it very unpleasant to see herself as an overweight person. She blocked this out by superimposing the image of a thin Constance. At the same time, part of her was aware of this self-deception. As a result, she became increasingly unhappy. Living alone, as she did, meant she couldn't run away from herself. There was no one else at home for her *but* herself.

Some people are unhappy because their self-image *never* lives up to their actual ability. They spend their entire lives working and living below their possibilities. These people do not like themselves. They are cheating themselves out of creative, interesting lives.

If this is your problem, substitute action for refusal. Assess your capabilities and don't settle for less than your full potential. An exaggerated sense of your importance will only make you unhappy. An inflated conception of your own abilities can lead to disaster. It will often result in personal embarrassment for you. You will be unhappy because you will never be able to feel appreciated by others. You will be unhappy because you won't feel that you are achieving what you planned.

Put aside all of your preconceptions about yourself. Try to step outside and away from yourself and see the *real* self-image. Wipe away those things which are clouding that picture.

Yes, you may find it painful. But, learning to live with yourself is a *growing* process. Growing is sometimes momentarily painful as we stretch ourselves to fit new dimensions.

THE SELF-IMAGE FOCUS

It may help you to think of this whole process much as being like taking a picture. If your lens is out of focus your finished picture will be blurred and out of focus.

Reality is your lens. The self-image is your picture. *To get results, get in focus.*

HOW TO MAKE A SELF-IMAGE PROFILE

When Constance had trouble with her false self-image, I suggested that she make herself a self-image profile. You can do the same for *your* self-image. Since we see ourselves both physically and mentally, we need to consider *both* of those aspects in our self-image profile.

On a piece of paper draw a quick sketch of what you think of as your body. Beneath it, list those physical features or physical characteristics which you think are outstanding.

Constance drew a picture that was almost like a stick figure caricature. Underneath she wrote such words as "thin," "tall," and "pretty." Another patient, a woman I was treating for anxiety, drew a picture of herself as a person with a large nose and feet. She used words like "ugly," "misshapen," and "deformed" for herself. In reality, she had an average proportioned figure with entirely normal features. She didn't like herself and felt unloved. She saw herself as ugly.

The next step is to go to a mirror. What do you see there? Look at the image in terms of physical characteristics only. *Pretend it is a stranger.*

Now, on another piece of paper, draw what you have seen. Prepare a *new* list of adjectives to describe the person in the mirror. You may have been seeing yourself mentally as in a funhouse mirror. The distortion isn't amusing when it makes it hard for you to live with yourself. Constance, for example, had to admit that what she really saw was a fat woman staring back at her. "Not only fat," she wrote, "but cross looking."

Now on a piece of paper list your personality traits and characteristics. After listing them, go over your life in your mind. Does your life reflect these traits? Can you provide evidence to prove the existence of those traits?

A man who had delusions of grandeur listed "generous" and "wealthy" as part of his characteristics. When pressed for evidence, he was forced to admit that there was none.

The self-image profile helps you to see *what* and *where* you are. It does *not* mean that you can not make a *new* self-image.

You *can* change your life and self-image to a more desirable one. You have the power, for the self *can* be remade since it is a created object.

HOW DID I GET THIS WAY? OR, CREATING THE SELF

Perhaps you will exclaim, as Constance did, "How did I get this way?"

As we said earlier, the self is made up of many things. Think of it as a mosaic. The pieces have come from several sources. Your parents have given you some; your ancestors have given you others. The group with which you live, work, and play add their bits.

In this mosaic are also found your moral ideas, your standards of conduct, your ethical rules. This is the part of your life which is administered by the *superego*. Our parents give us a set of rules. We constantly add to those rules. We also modify and change the rules. Sometimes we discard rules.

The superego is composed of our ego ideals and the conscience. The ego ideals system contains our goals, morals, ethics, and aspirations. The conscience is our system of prohibitions and inhibitions. This is our inner voice that cries, in varying intensity, "No! No!" when we think about or plan some action which is against the rules of the superego. This mosaic, which is very personal in nature, can be a harmonious, pleasing one. It can also be an ugly, unpleasant pattern. You will be happiest if you have learned to adjust the pieces in your mosaic so that they fit well together.

The self is a living, growing thing. You are a living, growing thing. *The two grow together.*

Much of your superego has already been established by the time you reach adulthood. Your self, some of which comes to you at birth and during your formative years, can be changed. It is your personal responsibility to decide what that self shall be. Your personality is *your* creation.

How would you describe your personality? Productive or sterile? Powerful or weak? Happy or miserable?

Nobody can change you except yourself. I can't change you. I can tell you how *you* can change yourself. The decision is your own. The action is your own. The results will be yours to enjoy.

FOUR *E's* THAT AFFECT YOUR CREATION OF SELF

The four *E's* that most affect your creation of self are (1) Experience, (2) Exposure, (3) Education, and (4) Environment. A discussion of these elements follows:

1. Experience—that daily living which you do or have done. It is made up of past experience and present experience. Much of your success in present experience depends upon what you have learned from past experience. Living successfully with yourself in the present is conditioned by your past. Your present and future happiness is often influenced by past experiencess.

2. Exposure—another part of your created self: exposure to other people; exposure to new ideas. *You are what you think.* If you don't feed your mind by exposing it to new concepts, it will become sluggish. You will be an uninteresting person. The more active your mind is, the more active your personality will be. The active personality is *fun.* The active personality is *happy.* The active personality is *likeable.*

3. Education—a part of your experience and exposure. Don't isolate yourself from people and ideas. Education is one process by which you gain valuable experience.

4. Environment—the life-style you have adopted as your own. You could not control your childhood environment. You *can* control and change your adult environment. You *should* change it if it means that a better self will come from the change.

Don't be indifferent to the four *E's*. Don't let them control you. You can be the master of your environment. You can select your experience. You can seek out the right exposure. You can learn from education.

How Conrad Used the Four *E's* to Create a New Self

"I'm just a failure, Doctor," Conrad said. "Nothing I do turns out right! I hate myself. I've even thought of suicide."

Conrad went on to explain that in the five years preceding his visit to me, he had suffered two almost overwhelming disasters. The small business he owned had failed. His marriage had ended in divorce.

"I seem to have had nothing but a series of problems in my life," he said.

Actually, he did not have several problems. Conrad had *one* problem—*himself.*

Along with other things, we talked about the four E's and how Conrad could use them to create a new personality.

When he came to me, Conrad was living in a small apartment which he did not like. The location was not close to his work. He spent long hours each day on the bus. The work he was doing was monotonous. It offered no possibility for advancement. He had taken the job when he was, in his words, "down on his luck."

Conrad had boxed himself into a negative environment. His first step in creating that new self would have to be to change his environment. Living with yourself, as I told Conrad, can be a difficult matter of adjustment. But living with yourself in surroundings you don't like can make it almost impossible.

Conrad changed jobs to one more suitable to his abilities and aspirations. He moved to a better apartment, close to his job.

We next tackled the other *E's* in Conrad's life. From his past experience he was able to learn why he had failed in business. He was able to honestly assess his marriage problems. Learning from the past made it possible for him to avoid making the same mistakes again.

At the same time, he began to build new creative experiences through education and exposure.

He admitted that his business failure had been partly caused by his lack of knowledge of retail trade practices. Since he was still interested in going into business, Conrad decided to take classes in business education.

Conrad's marriage had not succeeded because of a lack of shared interests and concerns. He had not known many girls when he made his decision to get married. Now, Conrad made an effort to enlarge his circle of friends.

Under the *E* of *Exposure,* Conrad joined a church adult group and a bowling league and became active in local political circles. In these groups, Conrad met girls who shared his interests.

Today Conrad once again owns his own business. He is successful in that and also in his second marriage. Conrad is a happy man. He can take pride in this creation of his new self.

You *can* create a *new* self. Apply the four *E's* to *your* life.

Don't box yourself in to a dull existence. Open up to expanded horizons.

HOW TO DISCOVER HOW YOU APPEAR TO OTHERS

An important part of your happiness comes from interpersonality relationships. This is how you get along with others. It is based not only on what you think of others, but also, and more important to you, it is based on what other people think of you. Part of your self-approval is the reflected approval of others. You are naturally anxious to appear your best before others. You want to win their approval. You need to know how they feel about you.

You can discover how you appear to others by seeing how they treat you. You can assume that their image of you is a positive one if they treat you with consideration and respect. A man who considered himself an expert in bridge was continually miffed because he was not asked to give advice or instruction. Obviously, others did not see him as a bridge expert.

Your self-image should agree, at least at major points, with the image others have of you. If you discover wide differences, there is a problem to be solved. Check both images for accuracy. If your self-image is at fault, correct it. If the outside image is, find out why. Then make necessary adjustments.

For example, you may be an expert in some field or skill but no one knows about it. Look for opportunities where you can demonstrate that ability.

If you have been fooling yourself and not others—*wake up to reality!* Face facts, and you will be able to face others.

THE THREE HIDDEN *L'S* IN SELF-ESTEEM

There may only be one *L* in the spelling of *self-esteem* but there are actually *three* important *L's* connected with that word. A person who has self-esteem has these three *L's*. He is aware of them. They are a part of his life.

The three hidden *L's* in self-esteem are (1) Loved, (2) Loving, and (3) Lovable. The person with self-esteem feels *loved* by one or more significant figures in his life. He also is *loving* toward one or more significant figures. This individual has a personality which is *lovable*.

Do *you* have the three *L's* in your life?

They are interdependent. You can not receive love until you develop the capability to give love. Being lovable means that you are the type of person that people reach out toward. They want to include you in their lives. They want to share with you.

BUILDING SELF-ESTEEM

You build self-esteem by doing your best. You learn your capabilities and live up to them. When you can, you *stretch* the limits of your capabilities. You do this through education, through work, and through thinking.

You build your self-esteem with self-respect. You like yourself as a person. You respect yourself for what you believe. Your actions are in harmony with your beliefs.

HOW TO LIVE ALONE AND KEEP YOUR SELF-ESTEEM HIGH

Living alone can be a pitiful trap for the careless. It can be misery for the person with low or little self-esteem. It can be dangerous for the emotionally immature.

You may be living alone because your spouse has died. You may be divorced. You may be alone and hoping to find a loved one or close friend. You may be living alone from choice.

In one sense, you are *not* living alone. You are living with *yourself.* You owe that self certain considerations.

Do you turn off your personality when you are home alone? That is just like turning out the light in a room. It becomes dark and dreary. You don't want to stay in a darkened room. You don't enjoy being with a darkened personality. Perhaps you want to eventually live with another person. Fine, but if you can't stand living with yourself, why expect someone else to put up with you?

Living alone can be a challenge to you. Accept that challenge. Make a happy home for *yourself.* Be *friends* with *yourself.* Learn to know and appreciate your good points. Develop your sense of humor. That humor will help you over dark hours.

Keep in mind that you can be an interesting person even when alone.

Tennyson expressed it this way:

Self-reverence, self-knowledge, self-control,
These three alone lead life to sovereign power.

How Sarah Learned to Be Happy While Living Alone

Sarah was very depressed when she came to see me. She burst into tears as she described her unhappiness.

"I hate living alone," she said as she cried. "Life is unbearable!"

Sarah had been living alone since her sister had married and moved to another town. She admitted that she did not make friends easily. "My sister was very outgoing," she said. "I more or less depended on her for our social activities."

When asked what kind of a person she would like for a friend, Sarah used words like "cheerful," "friendly," "creative," and "loving." Those same words, she explained, applied also to her sister.

"Do you think that such attributes as those made your sister more attractive to people? Were they factors in her getting married?" I asked Sarah.

She agreed that they probably were. But when I asked her which of these personality characteristics she had, Sarah was silent.

"Why don't you make those same characteristics yours also?" I asked.

I explained to Sarah that crying and wishing *never* brought happiness. Instead, you must plan a program of action and follow it.

Sarah changed her tears and whining for smiles and a cheerful demeanor. At first it was definitely a *pretend* situation for her. However, as her life became more interesting, those smiles were based on reality.

Since Sarah was shy, I suggested that she start by joining in some group activity where it would be easy for her to make friends. Following my suggestion, she enrolled in both craft and swimming classes at the local YWCA. Soon she was busy developing her new interest in ceramics.

A year later Sarah had the kind of personality she had once envied in others. Although she was living alone, she had so many friends and interests that this was no longer a problem.

"If I wished anything, Doctor," Sarah said, "it would be that I had stopped crying and gotten busier sooner!"

Yes, Sarah discovered that you can't sit still and *cry* yourself into popularity and happiness. You need to *get up, go out,* and *gather it in!*

SEX PROBLEMS OF LIVING ALONE

Sex is no longer hidden in the back roads of either society or the mind. Our present attitude that sex is a healthy part of normal living is a psychologically sound one.

It is important that you have meaningful encounters. The sexual relationship should not be a hasty one. It should not be one based solely on physical demands and necessity.

The sexual experience of a single person should not be much different than that of a married person. It may be more limited. It may be less frequent. But, emotionally, it should be *meaningful.*

HOW TO USE AND BENEFIT FROM YOUR CHOICE OF EGO IDEALS

Your choice of ego ideals shapes much of your self-esteem and helps make your personality. These ideals are part of your system of moral values. Your choice of them reflects your hopes and aspirations. You identify with your ego ideals; therefore, it is important that those you choose are suitable.

Our first ego ideals are usually our parents, older brothers or sisters, and teachers. As we get older, our circle of ego ideals becomes larger. We begin to identify ourselves with people beyond our immediate range.

Hero worship is common to all ages. Young people tend to admire popular singers, sports figures, and movie stars. Adults admire political leaders, successful businessmen, and outstanding scientists.

It is important that we do not permit early ego ideals to enforce ideas that are no longer applicable in our adult lives. Your parents may have been overly strict. Your teachers may have set standards beyond your reach. To continue to try to follow these ego ideals will only result in unhappiness and feelings of failure.

Avoid keeping or acquiring ego ideals that put you down. Your ego ideals should be a form of life adjustment. Don't let them trap you into guilty feelings. Reassess your early identifications. Discard those which are harmful or no longer valid. Choose new identifications which will help build your self-esteem.

Many people read the biographies of successful people and take their ego ideals from them. Success and creative living can be *caught* from others. Try it!

HOW TO CHOOSE THE SELF YOU WANT TO BE

If you are not satisfied with the self you have, change it. Choose the self you want to be. Choose the self that matches your ideal.

Take a good look at yourself. Be as objective as possible. Be fair to yourself. Be level-headed and unemotional. Decide what you want to keep in your present self or personality; decide what you want to eliminate; decide what you will need to add. Always keep in mind the ultimate self you want to become.

You may find it helpful to write these things down on paper. Make three columns headed *Keep, Eliminate,* and *Add.* These will form the basis of your change program that will result in your new self.

Finally, visualize yourself as the person you want to be. See yourself becoming that person. Follow the *Seven Steps in Remaking Yourself.*

SEVEN STEPS IN REMAKING YOURSELF

1. *Use your thoughts.* Deliberately use your thoughts to help you create and maintain a new self-image. Poor thinking means a poor image. Faulty thinking, as we have seen, means more unhappiness. Think of yourself in positive terms.

2. *Develop outside interests.* Don't spend your time thinking about yourself. *Get out! Get busy!* Develop a new hobby or sport. Brush up on an old skill.

3. *Reach out toward others.* You can not be happy living in a social vacuum. You need to have friendships and love in your life. You start in that direction by being friendly and lovable. Give some of your time to help others. Look for areas of volunteer work. Use some of your energy to help those less fortunate.

4. *Develop inner resources.* Just as a shallow river runs dry in time, a shallow person becomes empty. You can develop your resources by reading and studying.

5. Control your emotions. Dismiss old resentments from your mind. Forget old criticisms. Don't hang on to the memory of old disappointments. These negative emotions are one reason you were not happy with your old self.

Don't fill your emotional bank with new resentments, criticisms, or disappointments. They are like counterfeit money. They won't buy you one minute of happiness.

Yes, you may have disappointments, but don't over-emphasize them. If you can learn something from them, fine. Keep the lesson you learned and let it help plan your future. Throw away the rest of the experience.

6. Accept the challenges of your life. No matter what your life or occupation is, there are daily challenges for you. Don't back away from these challenges—accept them! They are ways of enlarging your horizons. Challenges are opportunities!

7. Consider yourself a winner. Don't sit around feeling sorry for yourself. The solution to bouts of self-pity and loneliness is to get busy with some mental or physical activity.

Think *victory* and *ways to achieve your goals*. Expect to reach your goals and you will find them within your reach.

A REMINDER

Only *you* can change your life by changing to the self you want to be. You can choose your *ego ideals*. You can set your goals. You can reach those goals. You can be a winner!

You can be happy with yourself. When you can live successfully with yourself, you will find that others will enjoy living with you also.

4

How to Develop Self-Honesty and
Maturity for Mental and
Physical Health

In our ethical culture, a high premium is placed on the principle of *honesty*. Honesty toward others is important but it can not compare with the importance of *self-honesty,* which is a necessity for real happiness.

You will see in this chapter how your entire emotional and mental health is influenced by your self-honesty. You will learn how self-honesty affects your business and professional success. You will learn how it affects the development of your relationships to others, including your marriage.

The degree of self-honesty you develop is an index to the degree of happiness and success you will enjoy.

DO YOU DARE TO TELL YOURSELF THE TRUTH?

How honest are you with yourself? Are you living in a dream world that you have invented? Perhaps you practice selective self-honesty. You select the things *you want* to hear about yourself, and ignore the unpleasant or unwanted facts. It's as if you cut out of a magazine a picture of someone you admire and pasted that picture over your mirror. Now when you look into the mirror, you say "That's me!" But it isn't you! It may be the *you*

you want to look like, but it is not your true physical image. You are deceiving yourself.

To have the wrong mental image of yourself based on self-deception and lies is just as wrong. It is foolish, and it will eventually make you unhappy.

Self-honesty is sometimes painful. Often, however, it is a way of raising your self-esteem. You can't *really* afford to deceive yourself.

Self-honesty *can* be learned. *You* can learn it. You can get positive results in your life through the practice of self-honesty.

THE EGO AND SELF-HONESTY

When you are not self-honest, you create a state of tension between the superego and the ego. The superego is the part of your unconscious which contains your ethical standards and your *guilt systems.* A popular name for all this is the *conscience.* These rights and wrongs come to us partly from our parents, partly from others who influence our thinking, and partly from our own experiences.

The ego is your eye on the world. It observes reality. The ego, however, is sometimes willing to make compromises with reality.

When the ego gets too much out of line with the demands of the superego, tension results. You become anxious and unhappy, and may even become physically ill. People recognize this problem when they say, "My conscience hurts." *They* are hurting because of this conflict between ego and superego.

YOU AND YOUR CONSCIENCE

You and your conscience are inseparable. You may have a weak conscience but it is there.

The conscience learned its moral codes. Therefore, the strength of your conscience depends upon your early moral training. Strict parents usually mean strict consciences in children. These implanted "no-no's" are carried on into adulthood. You may *do* things which your parents disapprove of but you will enjoy them *less.* Your conscience will give you nagging reminders from time to time—reminders that you are committing a "sin" or doing a "wrong" thing. These reminders, of course, are in terms of those early standards.

Your adult standards may be different in some respects from those given you as a child. Minor adjustments of conscience will not cause you anxiety or trouble. Major ones will. The man who smokes or has a cocktail even though his parents were opposed to tobacco and alcohol, will not be too tense. However, the man whose sexual conduct is in direct conflict with his early moral training, *will* suffer.

You have to learn to live with your conscience. You can do this best by analyzing your motivations. When you understand *why* you have certain desires, you can then make adjustments so they are compatible with your conscience.

The conscience is your personal policeman. Don't invite disaster by trying to bribe that policeman. Instead, make friends with your conscience; live happily with your conscience.

How Lee F. Learned to Stop Deceiving Himself

Lee F.'s family were worried about him. He was depressed and under medical care. He had started to complain of vague physical symptoms of pain. When he had trouble eating and keeping his food down, Lee's doctor asked me to examine him.

"There seems to be no organic cause," Doctor G. said. "Lee is actually a healthy man. I suspect now that his trouble is actually emotional."

Doctor G.'s diagnosis was confirmed after I had treated Lee over a period of time. Lee had never been able to be honest with himself. As a child he had been strictly raised by his parents. This strictness he had attempted to disregard as an adult. Unfortunately, he had not developed enough maturity to allow him to properly appraise his early moral standards in terms of his adult life.

His ego and superego were constantly at odds. This battle reached a climax soon after Lee brought home some office equipment from his firm and kept it for his personal use. A few months later when he was in financial trouble, Lee "borrowed" some money from his firm just as he had earlier "borrowed" the equipment.

Lee attempted to rationalize the taking of the money as he had the taking of the equipment. "I told myself that it was temporary," he admitted. "I also said that nobody was using the equipment. It wouldn't be missed. The firm was big so it wasn't as if I was borrowing or taking from some individual. The money I would pay back eventually but it wasn't needed by the firm at the time I was using it."

Yes, Lee tried desperately to rationalize his way out of his moral predicament. But his policeman-conscience kept shouting "stealing" instead of accepting the word-concept "borrowing" which he tried to use.

The tension generated by this conflict was too much for Lee. He could not face his lack of self-honesty, and tried to run away from the voice of his conscience by becoming physically ill.

Lee only became better when he learned to be honest with himself. He returned the money and the equipment to the company. He faced the realistic facts of what he had done.

Through treatment, Lee learned more about the psychology of his conscience and about the importance of self-honesty.Through self-analysis, Lee learned how to tell himself the truth.

If you have similar problems of self-honesty, you too can learn to be honest with yourself. Self-dishonesty is often responsible for your non-organic pains and other ills. Why suffer needlessly?

THE PSYCHOLOGICAL CONCEPTS OF SELF-HONESTY AND MATURITY

Self-honesty is an important criterion of maturity. The individual who persists in deluding himself is not acting as an adult.

We may smile at the unfortunate individual who considers himself to be Napoleon or God for we know the truth. We are embarrassed when someone we know claims to be something he is not. You bring embarrassment upon *yourself* when you behave in an immature way.

Children are immature. They have fantasies about who they are and what they can do. Children are frequently unrealistic. They may incorporate these fantasies into their lives and play as though they were true. A child can take his fantasy life very seriously.

A mature adult is aware of the difference between his fantasies about himself and real life. Self-honesty is working well from a psychological point of view when the ego and superego are in harmony.

How mature *are* you in relation to your self-honesty?

HOW TO TEST YOUR SELF-HONESTY

To test your self-honesty, you will have to step *outside* yourself. You have to see yourself *realistically*. You have to look at your motives *objectively*.

A simple way to test your self-honesty is to apply the *face-to-face* or *mirror* technique. You can either do this in your mind as a purely mental exercise or you can write the information on paper. (A patient of mine who is trying to develop his self-honesty keeps his self-honesty tests in a notebook.)

In the face-to-face technique, you list the things you are telling yourself about your own life, actions, and personality. These may be in relation to things you have done. It may be something you are doing. It may be actions you plan in the future. It may be desires or hopes. It may be personality characteristics. Study your list carefully and objectively. Now make a second list which will show you what the *real* facts are. It is important that you be very honest with yourself at this point.

Your two lists may match. Good! But where they don't match, you are attempting to deceive yourself.

As we go on through this chapter, you will learn how to *stop* deceiving yourself. You will learn how to look at yourself *honestly*.

HOW MENTAL BLOCKS CAN MAKE YOU DISHONEST ABOUT YOURSELF

Mental blocks are just that—blocks that you put in or across your mental processes. They are a means of denial, a defense mechanism. What people can not accept within themselves, they attempt to deny. This denial is a way of escaping psychic pain. It is a way of trying to cope with anxiety by rejecting reality.

Denial in the face of irrefutable evidence is difficult to maintain. It *can* lead to serious emotional or mental trouble.

The proverbial chip on the shoulder is sometimes indicative of a mental block, as in the case of the overly aggressive patient who insisted the world was against him. In particular, he claimed that his employers were "down on him." He had blocked out the fact that he was not qualified in any way for the job promotion he thought he should have.

In another case, a patient complained that his wife had deserted him. He had thrown up a mental block across the fact that he had physically abused her.

Do *you* have any mental blocks across the paths of your thought?

HOW THE MECHANISM OF REPRESSION MAKES US FORGET

Repression is the mechanism by which we attempt to forget and push out of our mind unacceptable or painful things. By repression, we are attempting to exclude them from our consciousness. These may be unacceptable or painful desires, memories or thoughts.

We all practice *some* degree of repression. Usually it is harmless. Forgetting the name of an unpleasant acquaintance is a form of repression. So is forgetting a dental appointment, or losing one's way enroute to a difficult or undesired appointment or meeting. Less harmless however are those repressions which keep you from an acceptance or proper evaluation of reality.

You may be repressing certain shortcomings which you have. But, repressing them will not change them. The short-comings or personality defects will still be a handicap to you. All you have done is *deny* to yourself that they exist.

Frequently people try to repress aggressive drives. They also try to repress forms of dishonesty. Some persons repress their instinctual sexual drives. Most individuals try to repress anti-social feelings.

Repression is accomplished by either an outright denial of facts or by rationalization. Denial is a pushing out of our minds what we refuse to acknowledge. The process of rationalization is more complex. It is a process of justification. It means finding an acceptable substitute reason for an unacceptable one. (In the case of Lee F. we saw how he attempted to talk himself into the idea that stealing was only borrowing.) Rationalization is a form of fictionalization. It rarely holds up well under stress.

How close to reality do you allow yourself to come? Are you

trying to fool yourself by denial of facts? Are you trying to rationalize your way out of painful or unpleasant things? Repression takes away your energy. It is a life-waster.

HOW TO LEARN TO LOOK AT YOURSELF HONESTLY

Looking at yourself *honestly* isn't easy. It is difficult; it takes real will power. You have to be willing to see the good *and* the bad. You have to be willing to admit to weaknesses as well as strengths. You have to be tough with yourself.

No one likes to own up to faults or weakness. However, you can change those *negative* aspects of your life into *positive* ones. Don't be afraid of looking at yourself honestly. Keep in mind that your ultimate result will be increased happiness. You will get more enjoyment out of life when you are honest with yourself.

Looking at yourself honestly is a *constructive* act, not a *destructive* one. You will learn more about this process in the section on self-analysis.

How Norman Learned to Look Honestly at Himself

Norman, a patient, wrote down in his self-honesty test that he expected to be a famous artist. This expectation had absolutely no connection with reality. After learning to look honestly at himself, Norman had to change that particular expectation. The real picture, as he later admitted, showed nothing like that occurring in his life. He had *no* artistic talent. Furthermore, he had made no plans to even study art. The truth was that he *wished* he were an artist.

John Adams was talking about politics when he said the following words about facts versus wishes, but they can be applied to everyday life situations:

"Facts are stubborn things; and whatever may be our wishes, our inclinations, or the dictates of our passions, they cannot alter the state of facts and evidence."

This was the thing that Norman had to accept. Facts must be faced. Actually, Norman was an extremely competent carpenter. This skill which he had, he was attempting to ignore. He became a well-adjusted individual when he learned to be honest with himself. He became a happy individual when he learned to take pride in his carpentry work.

Self-appreciation is a valuable by-product of self-honesty.

THE THERAPY OF SELF-ANALYSIS

Self-honesty can be learned by various approved psychological methods. You may want to have professional counseling and guidance. You may have a trusted friend who can be objective enough to help you evaluate your self-honesty.

Another method is through self-analysis. This book will help you to develop and use this skill, which is a way of getting better acquainted with yourself, of getting to know your unconscious self. It is probing beneath the surface of your apparent personality.

In the therapy of self-analysis, which will help you get a better understanding of your tensions and motivations, there are two self-analysis methods you can use. One is to *write* your self-analysis. The other is to *talk out* your self-analysis. Some people prefer to use a combination of the two.

You can decide which method is best for *you* to use.

HOW TO BE HONEST IN YOUR SELF-ANALYSIS

It is important to be honest in your self-analysis. If you are not honest, you are wasting your time; you are *cheating* yourself.

In your self-analysis you must include your fantasies We all lead a double life in the sense that we wish for things and for changes. People with imagination naturally tend to have a more highly developed fantasy life. *Repressing* these fantasies increases anxiety and intra-psychic tension. *Understanding* these fantasies in terms of reality will help you toward your personal adjustment patterns.

You will need to also know what *is* and what *can be*. To do this in your self-analysis, you will need to get an imprint from each of the three compartments of your mind—your *ego*, *id*, and *superego*. From your *ego*, you will get your imprint of *reality*. The *id* will show you your *desires* and *fantasies*. The *superego* will give you your *standards*. Taking all three into account will be a part of your self analysis program.

THE PLACE OF DREAMS IN YOUR LIFE AND SELF-ANALYSIS

Dreams are a special way of having fantasies at night. Although they are difficult to properly interpret, they can often furnish you clues to your repressed feelings. Dreams are a glance into your unconscious. They are, in a sense, messages from your unconscious.

Dreams contain unfulfilled wishes from the id. They will also contain some factors from external reality. This *day* residue is something which has particularly struck us. It often triggers the dream. Also present in dreams are elements from the superego. This may be an expression of our guilt feelings. Hidden in dreams are childhood and adolescent memories. These are usually difficult to discover.

Dreams are useful. They help us express repressed emotions, including hostile and aggressive ones. They serve as a kind of magic shop where we can obtain fulfillment of our wishes. Analyzing dreams can help us in our progress toward self-honesty. Studying our dreams will show us what our unconscious thinks and desires. Comparing dreams with your actual situation will help you to adjust your personality conflicts. By learning what emotions and ideas are just below the level of your conscious understanding, you are developing self-honesty. You are developing good emotional health.

Some individuals who use self-analysis, also keep a dream notebook in which they write down their dreams. They look for continuing themes and incidents that reappear in their dreams.

The dream is another kind of mirror in which you can see yourself.

HOW TO WRITE A THOROUGH SELF-ANALYSIS

Pick a quiet time. Select a place where you can sit and write without interruptions. *Relax!*

No one else should be present. What you write is for *your* eyes only. Thus, it should be easy for you to be honest about yourself.

In a sense, you are interviewing yourself. Try to be as objective as possible. If you have trouble getting started with your written self-analysis, you can start by writing an informal history of your own life. This autobiography can start with what you know about your ancestors. You may, however, want to start it with your own birth.

As you write about your life, you will include childhood memories and experiences as well as those of later years. You will want to list your accomplishments and achievements. If you are honest, you will also list your shortcomings and disappointments.

The point of this is to learn to know yourself better. Your written self-analysis should also identify your hopes and goals. Self-analysis may show you that you have exaggerated the importance and seriousness of some areas of your life to the neglect and detriment of others. Self-analysis will get a *balanced* picture of your life.

You may want to use the following *17-Point Personality Check List* in your self-analysis.

THE 17-POINT PERSONALITY CHECK LIST

To help you cover the many details in your self-analysis, you can follow these suggested 17 topics. These are points of reference to guide you in your self-analysis.

Answer these questions in your self-analysis. This may be in your written or vocalized self-analysis program.

1. What are my *outstanding* personality traits?
2. What are my *abilities* and *talents?*
3. How am I *using* those abilities and talents?
4. What are my *faults?*
5. Am I doing anything to *correct* those faults?
6. What are my *goals?*
7. Are my goals *realistic?*
8. What am I doing to *reach* those goals?
9. What are my real inner *motives?*
10. Do my motives and actions *match?*
11. Are any of my motives or actions in conflict with my *moral* standards?
12. Are there areas of my life which are *difficult* or *unsatisfying?*
13. What *seems* to be the *cause* of this difficulty or dissatisfaction?

14. Am *I* responsible for the problem?
15. What possible *solutions* can be found?
16. Is my *fantasy* life a help or a hindrance to me?
17. What do my dreams *reveal* about my inner life?

Your answers when viewed as a composite can arm you effectively for a sharp analysis of yourself.

HOW TO TALK THINGS OVER WITH YOURSELF

Some people prefer to talk out their self-analysis. You may prefer to do that.

Again it is important to select a quiet place where you will feel free to relax. You need an uninterrupted block of time. It need not be a long time. More important in your self-analysis program is the fact that you do it *regularly.* You may be able to take only a few moments each day for your self-analysis. But you should set aside *some* time each day for this period of self-examination.

Don't be evasive with yourself. Don't try to disguise your real feelings and attitudes. Don't become impatient. Don't get discouraged.

Self-analysis takes time. Self-analysis is a means of developing self-honesty.

SELF-HONESTY IS NOT SELF-CONDEMNATION

Self-honesty does not mean self-condemnation. Self-analysis time is not to be used to scold yourself. Rebuking yourself for your faults is a waste of your time. Blaming yourself for past failures or disappointments is another waste of time.

The whole purpose of self-honesty is to enable you to utilize the good in your personality while you change the undesirable traits. Self-honesty helps you *assess* your capabilities and *develop* your potentialities.

SELF-HONESTY TAKES TIME

It takes *time* to learn to be honest with yourself. It is not something you can achieve overnight. It is not something that comes out of one visit to a professional counselor or after one or two hasty sessions of self-analysis.

It is natural to run away from the unpleasant facts about ourselves. It is natural to want to avoid the disagreeable or the difficult. However, you can't *successfully* run away from yourself.

If you can't find time for yourself, you are probably trying to avoid self-confrontation. Decide *now* that you will take time to settle things with yourself. Put "know yourself" at the *top* of your list of things to do. *Start your self-honesty program this very day!*

PSYCHOSOMATIC ILLNESSES AND SELF-DECEPTION

Repression of a drive will result in either anxiety or some kind of body symptoms. This is especially true in regard to sexual or aggressive drives.

A repressed drive *will* find an outlet. You may think that you are repressing your desires and feelings successfully, but your body is telling you otherwise.

How Phyllis Overcame Her Rheumatism

"Some days I can hardly get around," Phyllis told me. "My rheumatism is so bad that it keeps me home most of the time."

Yet Phyllis' doctor had told me that he thought her rheumatism was *psychosomatic*. That is, it originated from some emotional cause rather than a physical cause.

Continued conversations with Phyllis brought out the facts that her rheumatism started when her engagement was broken. It also was worse on the weekends.

Phyllis was shocked when I asked her to tell me about her engagement. "I don't see what that has to do with my rheumatism," she complained.

Later, after treatment, Phyllis admitted that she was responsible for the broken engagement.

"My fiance and I quarreled over where we were going to live and how we were going to allocate our expenses," she said. "I told him I wasn't going to let him boss me around."

When her self-honesty was developed, Phyllis was able to see that her stubbornness had been the cause of the quarrels between her fiance and herself. She was also able to admit that she felt inferior to her friends because she was not married. Rheumatism became her refuge. It was her excuse for not being married. She even said to people that her health prevented her from leading a normal life.

Investigation revealed that a favorite aunt had had rheumatism. This was why Phyllis had selected it as her ailment.

Her rheumatism became worse on weekends when social activities for a young woman like Phyllis would be plentiful. Analysis brought out a repressed memory of an incident that occurred soon after her broken engagement.

"There was this big dance," Phyllis explained. "I didn't have a date. When a friend asked me if I was going, I was too ashamed to tell the truth. Instead I said I wasn't able to dance anymore because of my rheumatic condition."

Phyllis *did* dance again and do all the other things a young woman should do. She had learned to be honest with *herself.* Being honest with herself meant admitting that she was *using* rheumatism to avoid being honest about the past. Fortunately her doctor had seen the need for help before Phyllis had wasted too many years on her psychosomatic illness.

If you have an illness which your doctor says is *not* organic, study it in self-analysis. Like Phyllis, you may be repressing some emotion, incident, or guilt feeling. Why waste your time in unneccessary illnesses?

HOW TO DEVELOP YOUR TRUE PERSONALITY

Your *true* personality is there waiting for you. Discover it! Discover it now, *today!* Your happiness is directly related to this development of your true personality.

What do I mean by *true* personality? This is the personality that brings you the most happiness in your life. This is the personality that enables you to be successfully adjusted to life. You can learn about this personality of yours by being honest with yourself. You can change those personality traits which are keeping you from your best and full development as an individual.

You may have less talent and opportunity than your neighbor, but if you are honest with yourself and he deceives himself, you will be the happier person. You will be the more successful individual.

It is not how *much* you possess in personality traits, but how you *use* them. Your chances of using them to the best advantage will be greater if you are honest with yourself. The true personality that you discover can be the one you always wanted for yourself.

FIVE REWARDS FOR THE SELF-HONEST AND MATURE INDIVIDUAL

1. *Emotional stability to meet tense situations.* Tenseness can be caused by situations in your job or home life. Tenseness does not need to be disabling. You can, if you are honest with yourself, face these tense situations without undue anxiety. If you are emotionally mature, you will not experience prolonged periods of stress. Being self-honest means you can cope with tense situations. You will not exaggerate them but will be able to view them realistically.

2. *Better-adjusted mental health and corresponding physical health.* Elimination of self-deception from your life will make you feel better. You will not have to hide behind illnesses.

3. *Successful business and professional life.* When you can look at yourself honestly and realistically, you can look at the world that way also. Removing deception from your dealings with others will lead you toward success.

4. *Happy marriage and family life.* Self-honesty will help you to avoid many of the common causes of strife and anxiety in marriage and family living. When problems do arise, you will be able to handle them more easily.

5. *Popularity charm with others.* As a well-adjusted person, you will naturally attract others. Your pleasing personality will insure your popularity. The successful integration of your personality through self-honesty will give you the charm that others admire.

BUILDING SELF-ESTEEM WITH SELF-HONESTY

The more awareness you have of yourself, the happier you will be. You must have an awareness of the three compartments of your mind—the *ego*, the *id* and the *superego*.

As you develop in awareness and self-honesty your ego grows and expands. This expansion means greater happiness for you. You will feel better about yourself with this bigger self.

HOW TO FACE LIFE WITH A NEW ENTHUSIASM AND ENERGY

It is worthwhile to be frank with yourself. It is worthwhile to make an honest self-appraisal. The self-knowledge you gain will make you a successful individual. You will achieve emotional maturity.

The most important result, however, will be the increase in your *personal* happiness. You will find that you have a new enthusiasm for life. You will have more energy.

Self-honesty will give you this increased capacity for living. You will have an appreciation of yourself and your world.

A REMINDER

Self-honesty, which helps you to face up to reality, is the distinguishing mark of the mature individual.

Self-analysis is a way of developing self-honesty. It is a creative process. It is constructive.

Through self-honesty you can develop your true personality. Your desired happiness will come about naturally.

5

How to Create Better Mental Health
Through Your Daily Work
or Occupation

Although we place, and rightly so, great emphasis upon increased leisure, *work* is a *necessity.* We need the challenge of work in our lives. We need to be useful. We need to be creative.

Freud said, "True happiness is the capacity to love, work, and create." He saw that the individual had to express his capabilities, or he would not be happy.

These capabilities are best expressed through some kind of work. It can be *mental* work or it can be *physical* work. Many people find their *greatest* satisfaction and happiness through a combination of mental *and* physical work.

THE DANGERS OF NOT WORKING

The idea of not working appeals only to the immature person. Such an individual is uninformed about the true source and nature of his happiness. He is cheating himself.

What happens when you don't work? When you have capabilities and don't use them, a state of tension results. This tension is created between your ego and your superego.

Please remember that by "work," we mean a use of your talents and time to produce a desired product or result. Work may be in

81

an office, in a factory, or in the home. Work may be writing a book, painting a picture, or solving difficult mathematical equations.

Work is *accomplishment!*

THE IMPORTANCE OF CHOOSING THE RIGHT WORK FOR YOU

You can choose your work. It is important that you make the right choice and select work that is suited to your capabilities. The wrong work can cause tension and anxiety. It will make you miserable and bring you unhappiness.

In this chapter, I will show you how to choose your work wisely. Also, how to get the most out of your work situation.

You can have better mental health through your work.

Carlyle put it this way, "Blessed is he who has found his work; let him ask no other blessedness. He has a work, a life-purpose; he has found it and will follow it."

The right work is a permanent source of joy and happiness for you.

HOW TO DETECT THE ANXIETY STATE IN THE WORK SITUATION

If you come home from work feeling irritable or tense, you have anxiety symptoms. You may also suffer from excessive tiredness. This fatigue is a symptom of anxiety if it is out of proportion to the actual energy you have expended on your work. Indigestion, ulcers, headaches, and other physical ailments may be indications of anxiety connected with your work.

Sometimes that anxiety becomes so pronounced that you are unable to work. If your time away from work in the past year has been above normal, anxiety and tension may be the real causes.

How do *you* feel when you finish a job or a day's work?

TRANSFERENCE CONFLICTS IN THE WORK SITUATION

Transference is the transfer of childhood emotions to people other than the original recipients. It is a reproduction of those childhood emotions carried into adulthood and with new people. To put it more simply, it is as if you were putting on an old play with the same script but new actors. You, however, continue to play the same role.

Many times this transference process will result in conflict. Transfering your emotional relationship from *A* to *B* may produce anxiety. This will be especially true when *B* does not want to be a part of the emotional climate you have projected. Tension may also result when *B* does not understand his role and does not, therefore, respond the way you want or expect.

To go back to our play analogy, transference conflict results when the other actors do not want to use the script or do not understand it. In your work situation, transference conflicts are common occurrences. You may be attempting to relate to your boss as you did to your parents. Your previous relationship with your parents will color your relationship with your superiors at work. Sibling rivalry is often continued as an emotional transference toward your fellow workers. This rivalry which you had with your brothers and sisters can cause personality difficulties for you at work.

The work world is not an extension of your childhood. Are you still operating with the same set of emotions and values you had when you were a child? You can *change* those habits of transference. You are keeping yourself from good mental health by holding on to old emotions. You are keeping yourself from happiness.

How Arnold H. Overcame His Transference Conflicts

"I wish you would talk with Arnold H.," Mr. Smith said to me. "He is one of our best draftsmen but he just doesn't get along with the other men and women in the office."

Mr. Smith, who headed a large architectural firm, went on to say that he had been forced to pass over Arnold several times when promotions were being considered.

"I keep giving him one more chance," he admitted, "but I may have to let him go."

Arnold was a personable but nervous young man. He readily admitted that he was not happy in his work.

"I think I'm getting an ulcer," he said.

Analysis brought out the fact that Arnold was over-competing.

He had set the stage for rivalry and had proceeded to act in accordance with that false concept.

The reasons for his attitude were clearly revealed when he told me about his family life and childhood. Arnold was the youngest of five children. His parents had been very strict. His father had devised an elaborate system of competition among the children. This was then translated further into a complicated reward and punishment scheme.

As the youngest, Arnold found it difficult to compete. He resorted, therefore, to other attempts to curry favor and win rewards. When these methods failed, he gradually came to feel that all the others were against him. The harder he tried, the less he seemed to get.

By the time Arnold reached adulthood and went out to work, these attitudes were firmly fixed. All he did was to transfer his emotions from home to work. In this transference, Mr. Smith became his father; his fellow employees became his brothers and sisters.

The result of this transference was damaging to his career. It was damaging to his personality. It also robbed him of his happiness and peace of mind. It was affecting his physical health.

Through treatment, Arnold learned to change this pattern of transference. He put aside the emotions of childhood. He exchanged rivalry for cooperation. Mr. Smith reported that at first Arnold's fellow employees were skeptical of his new attitudes. Later, however, they accepted him on his changed values.

A year later, Arnold won a coveted promotion—a promotion he deserved not only for the quality of his work, but also for his pleasing personality.

Don't let transference conflicts keep you from achieving your best. Substitute cooperation for competition.

FOUR DANGER SIGNS OF FRUSTRATION IN YOUR JOB

There are four danger signs which indicate frustration in your job. These are signals to you of *hidden* problems—problems that are making you unhappy; problems that are causing tension within yourself. These tensions may find an outlet in one or more of these danger signs:

1. *Excessive smoking.* Is "lighting up" a *cover up* for frustration? Has your cigarette consumption gone up in response to your job pressures?

You can *not* smoke your way into solutions.

2. *Irritableness.* Irritableness of any degree or duration is always a sign of some emotional problem. In particular, it may be a sign of frustration.

3. *Increase in drinking.* Increased drinking will only *add* to your frustration. It will not permit you to do your best work. You will be left with an empty bottle and an empty life.

4. *Desires for escape.* Desires for escape are unrealistic. Running away does not solve any problems; it only postpones. There is always an eventual reckoning.

Escape may take the form of actual physical separation for periods of time from your work. It may also be more subtle in nature. Excessive sleeping or television watching are two common escape devices.

HOW TO HANDLE THE FOUR DANGER SIGNS

Any of the four danger signs can be handled by self-analysis. Try using this 15-point questionnaire to help you in your self-analysis:

1. Have I been smoking too much?
2. At what times do I smoke the most?
3. Has smoking helped me in any way?
4. Have I become more irritable?
5. Is this irritableness connected with my work?
6. Has this irritableness affected my personal relationships?
7. Has this irritableness warped my judgment?
8. Has my drinking increased?
9. Is alcohol becoming a refuge from work tensions?
10. Has increased drinking affected my work performance?
11. Do I waste time looking for a way out?
12. Do my desires for escape take the form of absenteeism, daydreaming, oversleeping, or persistent talking?

13. Do my desires for escape impair my efficiency?
14. What is the real source of my frustration?
15. How can I best solve that frustration?

You may find that you are in the wrong job. You may find that you have been putting emphasis on the wrong things.

An honest attempt to discover the *source* of your frustration is the first step toward learning to handle that frustration—and learning to handle it *successfully.*

How Ted Applied the 15-Point Questionnaire to His Job Frustration

Ted, an engineer, was suffering from several symptoms of anxiety and tension when he consulted me. I asked him to fill out the *15-Point Questionnaire.* After completing the questionnaire, he was able to pinpoint the *source* of his frustration—lack of preparation for his new assignment. He then thought of possible *solutions.*

His answers looked like this:

1. No
2. -
3. -
4. Yes
5. Yes
6. Yes
7. Yes
8. Yes
9. Probably
10. Possibly
11. Yes
12. Absenteeism
13. Yes
14. I am not sure how to do my present job assignment.
15. By admitting my uncertainty and seeking help through consultation with more qualified engineers. Also by study and reading.

Ted followed his own suggestions. His frustration disappeared;

so did his anxiety symptoms. He no longer drank too much or stayed away from work.

"My wife says she hardly recognizes my pleasant disposition," Ted reported. "I know I feel like a new man!"

HOW THE WRONG JOB CAN CAUSE EMOTIONAL OR MENTAL PROBLEMS

The wrong *job*, the wrong *place* or the wrong *time* can cause serious emotional or mental problems.

What is the wrong job? You are in the wrong job when you are working at a job solely because of external obligations. You are not fulfilling your true capacities. This will cause conflict within yourself and you will find yourself in a state of inter-psychic tension.

What is the wrong place? You are in the wrong place when the physical environment of your job causes tension or anxiety. You may be working in too small an office or firm. You may feel lost in a very large company.

What is the wrong time? You are in the wrong time slot if you are not prepared to do your job. This matter of preparation can be one of education, training, or psychological reactions.

The case of Ted was a good example of this. He really enjoyed being an engineer. The firm that employed him was one that had pleasant working conditions. But Ted was in the wrong time for his particular job. It was only *after* he had taken more instruction that he was able to get over his job-related emotional problem.

How Bob and Art Solved Their Job-Related Emotional Problems

Bob and Art worked side by side in the office of a large food processing plant. They spent a lot of their time griping instead of doing their work. Both men were unhappy, but for different reasons. They both blamed their feelings of depression and tension on "working conditions." In reality, the plant where they worked was modern and offered many advantages to the employees.

Investigation revealed that the sources of their job-related emotional problems were *wrong job* and *wrong place*. Bob was in the wrong *job*. Art was in the wrong *place*.

Food processing and office work bored Bob. He had taken the job because it paid well and the company had many fringe benefits such as an excellent pension plan. Working for the remote future, however, was no pleasure for Bob whose *main* interest was in automobiles. Since he had an outgoing personality, it was suggested to him that he might achieve more happiness as an automobile salesman.

Bob accepted this suggestion and became a very successful salesman. A few years later he owned his own automobile dealership. More important than his material success was his personal happiness. Bob had found it through finding the *right job.*

Art liked the work at the office but he intensely disliked the long drives to and from work each day. It was not feasible for him to move his family closer to his work because the food processing plant was located in a highly industrialized area.

Fortunately, Art was able to secure a bookkeeping job with an insurance firm which was close to his home. Once the tensions caused by commuting were removed from his life, Art became a happy man. He had found the *right place.*

PSYCHOSOMATIC ILLNESSES AND ACCIDENTS CAUSED BY WORK

Every year there are great losses in time and money because of illnesses and accidents caused by work. Many of these illnesses are psychosomatic in origin; many of the accidents can be attributed to emotional causes. Anger at the boss or supervisor is a direct invitation to an accident. Any kind of an authority struggle is apt to result in an injury.

I remember a case of a man who had been raised by a strict father with whom he had not gotten along. He carried this resentment of his father over into a resentment of authority. A strict boss called forth all of his old feelings about his father. He had a tendency to exaggerate the role and importance of the boss. He saw aggravation where none existed.

On one occasion when ordered to move a small motor, he resented this order. As he moved it, his thoughts of anger became so strong that his good sense was overpowered.

"All I could think of was to kill the guy," he said later. "I just saw red!"

Fortunately for the boss, my patient had also a strong sense of "no" implanted in his superego. In his anger, he dropped the motor on his own foot instead of throwing it at the boss. He suffered a broken foot as a consequence of his action. This broken foot with its pain also served to punish him, in his mind, for his wicked desire to kill the boss.

Any emotional conflict caused by work situations can produce illnesses. Ulcers, headaches, gastro-intestinal upsets are frequent psychosomatic expressions of unhappiness in work.

What about *your* health and accident record? Is there any connection between your attitude toward your work and your health problems? Perhaps you need to change to one of the three "rights"—*right job, right place, right time.*

HOW TO DETERMINE WHY YOU CHOSE YOUR PRESENT JOB

Making the proper choice of a job or profession is important. That choice will determine your *level* of happiness, and your *degree* of good emotional and mental health.

If you are having emotional problems related to your work, you need to examine your reasons for being in your job or profession. Think back to when you first made your decision. Why did you choose the field you did?

Perhaps you will discover that you didn't make a *real* choice at all. Perhaps you simply "fell" into your present occupation.

Test your choice by using the Ten-Point Work Choice Scale.

THE TEN-POINT WORK CHOICE SCALE

Look at your past decision to choose your particular profession or occupation and check which of these ten reasons were behind your choice. You may have several reasons for your choice. Indicate them in the order of their importance to you in making your decision.

1. Motivation
2. Identification
3. To please others
4. Salary
5. Glamour

6. Prestige
7. Aptitude
8. Skill
9. Fear
10. Chance

As part of your self-knowledge program, take a second look at that list. This time indicate what reasons you would use at the *present* time in choosing a new profession or occupation.

How well do the two lists match in indicators? A wide difference will show you the possible source of your unhappiness in your work.

A CLOSER LOOK AT THE TEN-POINT WORK CHOICE SCALE

Now take a closer look at these work choices. As you do, keep in mind your *own* choices. Keep in mind both your *past* and *present* choices.

Motivation is the highest type of work choice. This is often the idealistic or altruistic choice. Frequently persons who go into religious, medical, or social work make their choice because of this strong feeling.

Identification is often the prime reason for choosing a lifework. This is identifying with parents or other adults and selecting work identical or similar to their work. Often this is a mistake, for it does not represent the true or real choice. Little boys quite naturally say they want to be firemen or doctors when they grow up. But their ideas change as they learn more about the world and themselves. However, it is more difficult to change those ideas if your father is a fireman or there have been generations of doctors in your family.

Choosing your occupation *to please others* is closely allied to a choice through identification. Many youngsters choose their future work to please their parents. While this may be work they enjoy and can do, sometimes it is not suitable. A profession that you choose to please your father or mother may make you unhappy.

Occasionally a young husband will change his lifework to please his new wife. If this change is one in which he can concur, it will be good for him. If not his true choice, he and eventually she will be miserable.

Salary is a mistaken choice. Money by itself will not bring you happiness. Money *plus* having the *right* job will bring you great happiness.

Glamour and *prestige* are work choice traps for the immature. Any work when suited to your capabilities and needs has glamour for you. Doing your particular job best will give you the prestige you need.

"I'm a poor lawyer and I don't really like the legal field," a patient confessed to me. "I decided to become a lawyer because it seemed like a profession with lots of prestige. I wish now I had become a history teacher. That was my first choice, but I talked myself out of it!"

Aptitude and *skill* are good choices to make. If you choose a lifework which you can do and understand, you will automatically insure your success and happiness. On the other hand, spending your life in a job or profession for which you have no skill, knack, or interest is to doom yourself to failure and misery.

Fear dictates some people's choice. They do not have faith in themselves. They have low self-esteem.

"I wanted to go into my own business," another patient told me. "I had a chance but I was afraid to take it. Instead I took a job with a big company. I've always regretted that decision!"

It was that regret that had brought him to my office. It was that regret that was giving him headaches and insomnia.

Chance is the lazy way out. This is a negative kind of choosing. If you have a tendency to drift into jobs, you are not doing your best.

The happiest person is the one who chooses his lifework on the basis of *motivation, aptitude,* and *skill.* In that case, *salary, glamour,* and *prestige* come along naturally.

IT'S NEVER TOO LATE TO CHANGE YOUR CHOICE OF WORK

It is *never* too late to change if your present work choice is causing you unhappiness. If you have emotional or mental problems caused by your work—*change that work!* Take a good look at what you want to do. Take a good look at the prospects of doing it. If what you want to do is within your capabilities, do it!

It takes only *one* step to get started. Taking that one step can bring you the happiest years of your life. The world is filled with men and women who had the courage to stop in midstream and change directions.

Make your plans now! Carry them out!

FINDING THE LEVEL OF YOUR WORK CAPACITY

You will be happier when you are working to the fullest of your capabilities. However, you may need help in finding the level of your work capacity.

Frustration results when you are *not* operating at your highest capacity. Unhappiness, emotional problems, and physical illnesses may come about because of your frustration.

The person who is frustrated in his work owes it to himself to go and have psychological testing to determine his *natural* aptitudes. An *aptitude-interest test* may reveal some surprising and valuable things—things that will help in constructive vocational planning.

SATISFYING THE DEMANDS OF YOUR EGO IDEALS AND FULFILLING YOUR WORK RESPONSIBILITIES

Chronic frustration can be created if you set your standards through your ego ideals too high.

Think of your standards and capabilities on a scale. If your *standards* register at ten and your *capabilities* register eight, you will be unhappy and frustrated.

It is better for you to learn what you *can* do. *Accept* what you can do and build your self-esteem upon this. Once you have learned to accept the limits of your capabilities, you can investigate ways of *stretching* those limits. Where you can not do this, you can simply do your very best in terms of your capabilities. Doing your best will mean satisfaction and will bring you *lasting happiness*.

HOW TO BECOME PSYCHOLOGICALLY ORIENTED
TOWARD YOUR WORK

It is important to be psychologically oriented toward your work. If you don't like the work you are doing, you are headed for trouble. You will eventually transfer that dislike to others and to yourself.

Having the job most suited to your needs and capabilities is the first part of your psychological orientation. We will call that Number 1.

Number 2 is total immersion in your job. Learn all you can about *what* you are doing. Learn all you can about *why* you are doing what you do. Relate your activities to the activities of others. See where *your* part fits in the overall pattern. This is especially important when you work in a large company.

Number 3 is setting goals. Don't be content just to do your job day after day. Keep a personal performance record. Strive for increased productivity in all that you do. Have a set of goals. Keep reaching toward achievement.

Number 4 is stimulation through achievement. Review your progress at regular intervals. Note your various accomplishments and achievements. Doing this will help you build self-esteem and will encourage you to reach your future goals. Your motivation in your work will be kept at a high level.

Seeing where you have come from and what you have done makes it possible for you to believe in what you are going to continue to accomplish.

THE PRICE OF ADVANCEMENT AND HOW TO PREPARE
YOURSELF FOR IT

Strangely enough, some individuals have *more* emotional problems after reaching a desired plateau of advancement. They may become neurotic. They often develop psychosomatic illnesses.

Since success will be your desire, you can learn to prepare for it in advance. When you achieve that desired success, you will be emotionally able to handle it.

Frequently there is guilt associated with getting what you want. However, you should learn to accept and enjoy what you get. You can enjoy your success without suffering. You can have advancement in your work without conflict in your personal life. If you always follow ethical rules, you will have no fears after reaching the top. You can look others in the eye without flinching if you have not been unscrupulous in your actions.

Hard work and moral conduct are the best guidelines for you to follow in your upward path. Don't destroy your future happiness by using cheapening shortcuts in your drive toward success.

You will not be lonely or feel guilty when you are at the top if you have continued to develop your inner resources.

HOW TO CORRELATE YOUR INNER DRIVES WITH THE DEMANDS OF YOUR WORK

Your inner drives should be in harmony with the demands of your work. You should learn to keep these inner drives under control.

Work is an application of all of your ego functions. Your instinctual functions, which are your inner drives, should not be allowed to interfere with your work life and work patterns. These inner drives come from your id. We have already seen how conflict between the id and ego can cause interpsychic tension. You can avoid this tension by correlating and sublimating your drives.

Your pleasure-loving and pleasure-seeking drives should be satisfied during your coffee breaks or recreational periods. You should not expect to satisfy your love life or erotic demands during working hours.

You can control your aggression drives and use them in your work. Too much emphasis on aggression, however, will bring you into conflict with others. Find and use your happy medium.

Your success or failure in your work will depend on your willingness and ability to manage your inner drives. *Self-indulgence means self-destruction.*

ACHIEVING PERSONAL HAPPINESS AND SATISFACTION
FROM YOUR WORK

Personal happiness and satisfaction can come to you because of your work. Choose your work wisely. Become *involved* in your work. Your greatest happiness will come from knowing that you have done a good job.

No matter *what* you choose as your occupation or profession, it can bring you happiness. You give dignity to any work by the interest and attention you give to it.

A REMINDER

You have the power to get the most out of your work.

Eliminate frustration by becoming involved. Eliminate tension by having pride in your work.

Set up goals for yourself. Keep track of your achievements.

Don't be afraid of work. Demand the best from yourself, and collect the reward of happiness..

6

How to Use Leisure to Lengthen

Your Healthful Life

Leisure is a necessary part of your life. Leisure is important for your happiness; it is essential for your good mental health; it helps you to have good physical health. However, it is not enough just to *have* leisure time, it is *using* leisure time that is important.

You need to use your leisure time wisely. You need to plan your leisure activities. In this chapter I am going to show you how to get the best *personal* value out of your leisure.

PSYCHOLOGICAL PITFALLS TO AVOID IN LEISURE

Some people interpret leisure as laziness. This is one psychological pitfall to avoid. Yes, leisure *is* relaxation. But a continual program of "do-nothing" will *not* provide the needed relaxation.

At the opposite end of the scale is the psychological pitfall of overactivity. When you make work or duty out of your leisure activities, you are shortchanging yourself.

Planning recreational activities that are not your *true* choice is another pitfall. Don't choose or plan leisure time projects that please other people and not yourself. Frequently a married partner will force a hobby or activity on his or her spouse. To avoid an argument, the hobby is pursued. But it is not real relaxation when the individual would really prefer to be doing some other thing.

A psychological pitfall to avoid is attempting recreational

activities which are too difficult to accomplish. More tension and anxiety will result from this unwillingness to live within the limits of your capabilities.

Failure in relaxation can be as serious in its effects upon your life as failure in any other area.

How Edward A. Solved the Problem of His Hobby

Edward A. was a businessman who suffered from many symptoms of tension. He held an executive position which required long hours, considerable concentration and some travel.

"I can't seem to relax," he told me. "Even though I'm tired, I don't sleep well. My wife says I'm too jumpy. I enjoy my work but maybe I do spend too much time thinking about business matters."

When I asked him if he had a hobby, he hesitated. Finally he admitted that he did have a hobby—woodworking.

"But I don't really enjoy it!" he burst out saying.

Further conversation revealed that Edward's *wife* had actually selected this hobby *for* him. It was she who had purchased the tools, instruction books, and plans. She had even ordered the wood for him!

"I know she meant well," he explained, "but I never have been interested in any kind of craft work. And I'm not particularly good at it either."

Investigation showed that Edward's wife was forcing him to adopt the same hobby her father had pursued. Her father, however, enjoyed woodworking.

Edward confessed that he really wanted to collect stamps. This was a hobby he had enjoyed as a boy. It was a hobby he could indulge in while traveling.

"My wife says stamp collecting is silly and a waste of time," he said. "You know, Doctor, sometimes when I am on a trip, I go to a stamp store and just look."

Edward's leisure time was not really his own. He needed to relieve his tension in the way best suited to his interests. His wife had to accept the fact that her husband and her father were not necessarily interested in the same things. She had to learn to be willing to let her husband make his *own* decisions about his leisure.

This case had a happy ending because she was willing to do this. Edward enjoyed his stamps, and as a result he began to feel better and was more relaxed.

HOW THE FRUSTRATIONS OF CHILDHOOD ARE REFLECTED IN ADULT USE OF LEISURE TIME

The frustrations of our childhood are reflected in our adult lives. They influence our adult choices and our daily living patterns. They can control the way we, as adults, use or spend our leisure time.

If as a child, you were not encouraged to make constructive use of your leisure time, you will not be able to do so as an adult.

"I have nothing to do," is the whine of the undirected child. That child is discontented. That child is frustrated. That child is unhappy.

"I just kill time," is the admission of that child become an adult. That adult is *discontented*. That adult is still *frustrated*. That adult is *unhappy*.

The adult who never was allowed to develop his own individual creativity will have to learn that process for himself. The child who was not permitted to select his own hobby or form of fun will need direction as an adult. If direction is not provided, he will become a chronic time-waster. He will continually feel frustrated in his life.

Are you playing in the shadows of your childhood? Change the influence of those frustrations into enjoyable fulfillments.

How Mike Learned to Stop Competing with His Children

"Our home is always in an uproar," complained Ellen, Mike's wife. I have five children, but actually I have six for Mike behaves just like a child!"

She went on to explain that Mike insisted on taking over all the leisure time activities in their household and used them to compete with his children. He had developed a very aggressive attitude, and insisted on dominating the family recreation periods.

"From parcheesi to ping-pong, he turns the games into nightmares of competition. No one has a good time. I don't think it is good for the children," Ellen told me.

Although, as I assured her, some competition was healthy and desirable, an *excessive* amount could be harmful. Too much competition in a basically friendly situation could lead to interpersonal tension.

Mike had been dominated as a child by his grandparents with whom he lived. They did not allow him to pal with other children or to engage in games or sports.

Frustrated in his natural desires and inclinations, Mike waited until he was married and a father to attempt to satisfy those frustrations. He was reliving his boyhood with his children but on his terms.

Mike's aggressive and competitive tendencies were eventually directed away from his children and their games. He took up bowling and golf, in which he participated on an *adult* level with other adults.

THE EFFECTS OF IMMATURITY IN YOUR RESPONSES TO LEISURE

Immaturity can have an adverse effect on your capacity to enjoy your leisure.

There are six kinds of immature attitudes toward leisure which may not only spoil your fun and good times, but may also spoil your personality. These six are the most common ones that we see. Do you have any of them?

1. *Aggression.* Aggression is an *id* drive. Unless controlled, it makes you have antisocial reactions.

Aggression is a drive for mastery. It may be expressed in violent outbreaks of temper, general irritability, destructive behavior, or attempted domination of others. In most cases, there is a highly developed sense of competition coupled with an overwhelming desire to win.

Mike was an example of this form of immature response to leisure.

2. *Poor Sportsmanship.* The bad loser is reacting in an immature or childish way. We expect this of children because they are still extremely self-centered. We expect adults, however, to know and accept the fact that not everyone can be a winner.

3. *Timidity.* Timidity, when it keeps people from exploring all the possibilities of their leisure, is an immature response. This

timidity may be a fear of failure. It is an indication of low self-esteem.

"I don't know how," "I can't learn," and "People might laugh at me," are all excuses offered by timid individuals. They cheat themselves out of some of the best experiences of their lives.

4. *Perfection.* Perfection, while a desirable attribute in most instances, becomes an immature response when carried to an extreme. Too much emphasis on perfection can keep you from enjoying your leisure. While you may want to strive to improve your technique or skill, you should not make this the central issue.

5. *Guilt.* For many generations we have lived in a work-oriented society. Leisure was rare, and was reserved for a fortunate few. Life for the average person was hard. Life was short. There was no time for play.

Our modern mechanized society has changed all this. Technology has given us free time.

Some people, however, still retain vestiges of these guilt feelings about idleness. This is no longer a valid and mature response to leisure. Complex society now demands of us, for our survival, creative leisure as well as a certain number of work hours.

6. *Wrong Proportionment.* Proportionment is an act of balance. It is having the right amounts of work and leisure in your life. The wrong proportionment is immature.

Just as a child wants to play all day, an adult who neglects his work for his leisure is not being realistic. On the other hand the individual who can not find time to fit leisure activities into his busy schedule is immature. He is concentrating on only *one* aspect of his personality and life and is cutting himself out of another dimension.

If your leisure is not relaxing, you may have one or more of these immature attitudes. If your leisure time is only a *small* fraction of your day or week, you are doing yourself an injustice.

Take a *good* look at your leisure. Does it make you more tranquil or more tense? You may need to change some of your responses to leisure.

How Mrs. L. Learned to Change Her Response to Leisure

When Mrs. L.'s family brought her to me, she was in a state of collapse. She had been known as one of the busiest women in her community. She was a civic leader as well as active in church and social circles.

"Mother never sat down," her bewildered daughter explained. "She was always busy. Now she just seems to have lost interest in everything. She says she doesn't have any energy."

Analysis revealed that Mrs. L.'s father had been extremely strict. He did not believe in any form of leisure. He had punished his children whenever he saw them idle. Even after she had married and left her father's house, Mrs. L. could not get away from this attitude toward leisure. Although she saw how wrong her father was in his ideas, she could not change. She wanted to but could not.

This conflict in her mind between what she really wanted to do—relax and enjoy life—and her father's dictum that life and work were synonymous, finally proved to be too much for her. Her mind and body rebelled.

Treatment finally brought Mrs. L. to the point where she could discard her previous notions about leisure. She had mistakenly thought that to go against her father's ideas was a repudiation of him as a person. She learned that this was not so. Her respect and love for her father remained the same.

Each generation must face this problem for itself. Times *do* change, and the prohibitions and taboos of one age become acceptable to another age. As I mentioned earlier in this chapter, there has been a marked change in our whole attitude toward leisure and recreation.

HOW REGRESSION HELPS US TO RELAX

Regression, which helps us to relax, is an important part of our leisure. It means returning to earlier and less mature forms of behavior. The person who can not regress becomes compulsive and rigid.

Although regression in itself is a form of immaturity, the *proper use of it* is a sign of *maturity.* There are times when you can and should act silly. There are times when you should be able to move backward in time to a more primitive state in your development.

What happens is that we put to rest temporarily the more sophisticated and intellectual powers of our ego. This is a way of recharging our emotional and psychological batteries.

You should learn to be flexible enough to go from your work and responsibilities into a more primitive state. The busy executive who takes a week off to go on a camping and fishing trip is making the right use of regression when he wears old clothes and does not shave or become too concerned about cleanliness.

It is healthy to be silly at *appropriate* times. Older women who, when they get together at purely female social occasions, giggle and exchange confidences like young girls, are actually using regressive methods to relax from their lives of domestic responsibility.

Are you able to relax through the use of regression? When was the last time you let yourself go and *laughed?* Too much dignity can mean a constricting dullness in your personality.

Don't be afraid of regression. Use it in a mature way.

HOW TO PLAN CONSTRUCTIVELY FOR YOUR LEISURE TIME

Don't let time slip through your fingers like sand. Don't let your leisure time become blank, arid periods in your life, but be prepared to use that leisure time *constructively.*

George Herbert, the 17th-century English minister and poet, said, "He hath no leisure who useth it not."

Your leisure is your opportunity to refresh yourself emotionally and mentally. It is true that "All work and no play makes Jack a dull boy." It is also true that all work and no play will make Jack a *sick* boy.

Plan *ahead* for your leisure time. Don't wait and then waste time wondering what you should do.

FIVE THINGS TO CONSIDER WHEN PLANNING TO USE YOUR LEISURE TIME

You can make your leisure times more enjoyable if you will take these five things into consideration.

1. *Your special inclinations.* If you prefer to be a spectator rather than an active participant, keep that in mind. Don't plan on

going bowling if you would really prefer to watch a football game. The opposite is of course also true. You will only become fidgety and tired if you prefer *active* recreation and try to settle for *passive* avocations.

2. *Admit your limitations of interest.* There are as many interests as there are people. Don't try to pattern your interests after the interests of someone else. Develop your own and be willing to admit that there are limitations to your interests. Don't be ashamed of those limitations. If you go to the opera when you really have no musical interests and would prefer a good movie, you are not using your leisure properly. You may fool some of your friends but you aren't really fooling yourself.

3. *Length of time available.* You will be unhappy if you don't plan for the block of time that is available for your leisure. You will be frustrated if you plan more than can be done. *Hurry is not relaxing.*

If you have one hour of *time,* plan one hour of *leisure,* not *two.* When planning a trip, take into account the time that must be spent getting to and from your destination. This is particularly important in short trips.

4. *Money to be expended.* Some leisure time activities cost money. This may be in the form of admission tickets, food purchases, rental or purchase of equipment, transportation or other fees. Don't plan a leisure activity or hobby which is out of line with your budget. Remember that some hobbies such as photography require not only an initial outlay of funds but also a continuing expense for materials.

5. *Seasonal possibilities.* Consider the season when you plan your leisure. There are recreations which are more enjoyable and practical in summer than in winter. There are others which are definitely cold weather recreations. Take advantage of the seasons. Do some of those special seasonal things.

HOW TO OVERCOME SUNDAY NEUROSIS AND HOLIDAY DEPRESSION

Some individuals are unable to plan constructively for their leisure time because of an emotional block. This emotional block is often caused by Sunday or holiday depression. This depression, which can incapacitate people, is so common that Freud coined the term *Sunday neurosis*. Out of ten acquaintances I know, at least four suffer from some form of Sunday neurosis.

Sunday or holiday depression occurs when you are too dependent upon your daily life and work routines. When that rhythm is broken by a Sunday or holiday, you become depressed. You feel lost and let down. You are unhappy. Brooding takes the place of organized work. Worry fills in the empty hours.

Do you dread Sundays? You can change your attitude and your Sundays. Make the effort to climb out of your morass of depression. Build up your inner resources. Challenge yourself to plan a day of enjoyment. Keep *busy*.

One method which has proved very successful is to plan some activity with another person. It is more meaningful if *you* do a major share of the planning. You might also try inviting someone over for dinner. Attending a religious service may be helpful in getting yourself out of your Sunday rut.

Redirect your thoughts. Widen your outlook. Be willing to share with others. Look for recreational opportunities.

How Brenda Overcame Her Sunday Depression

"I hate Sundays!" Brenda said. She then burst into tears as she described to me how miserable her Sundays made her feel.

"Sundays are so depressing. I have nothing to do," she explained. "Sometimes I feel like there is nothing ahead in life for me. By Sunday night I am all tense."

Brenda should have been enjoying her Sundays. She was a young woman, employed as a secretary in a large company. Sunday was her main day of recreation and fellowship. This was the one day on which she could really get away from it all and relax.

Talking with her revealed that she depended on her company work and atmosphere to carry her through her own life. She had ceased to develop her own inner resources.

Brenda reluctantly agreed to plan a Sunday activity sheet and stick to it.

"Make a social-recreational calendar for yourself," I said.

With my help, Brenda planned her next Sunday. At first she seemed unable to think of any activity to write on her calendar. Following my suggestions though she finally came up with the following items:

Attendance at a church service Sunday morning, followed by lunch at a restaurant. In the afternoon, a tour of the local art museum. Dinner at home and attendance at a play being given that evening by the Community Theater Group.

As a final suggestion I said to her, "Don't be afraid to *smile* at people."

Brenda reported a week later that her Sunday had been a success.

"I was tempted to give up after dinner and stay home," she admitted, "but I remembered my promise to you to stick it out. I'm certainly glad that I did for I met a very nice lady who works in my same office building. She is active in the Community Theater and has asked me to help her committee with the next play."

Brenda learned that Sundays need not be times of suicidal unhappiness. She redirected her thoughts, widened her outlook and developed her own resources.

If you have a problem with Sundays, plan a social-recreational calendar for yourself. You will be surprised at the changes in your life and thinking when you *replace panic with planning*.

THE PSYCHOLOGICAL IMPORTANCE OF CREATIVE IDLENESS

Leisure can be creative and beneficial. It can give you a renewed interest in life. Your mind and your body both receive benefit from the change of pace.

Ovid, the famous Roman poet, summed it up in these words, "Leisure nourishes the body and the mind."

Leisure gives you a rest from your work. In addition, the creative use of this leisure or idleness can prepare you for future constructive work. After a period of creative idleness, you will find that you think more clearly. You can return to your work with new vigor. You will have more enjoyment in your work. You will exercise better judgment. You will have better physical coordination. You will be happier.

EIGHT WAYS TO USE LEISURE HOURS

So many people have trouble in deciding what they might like to do that they end up doing nothing. Here, however, is a list of eight ways to use leisure hours. These are suggestions to make leisure more enjoyable.

Not everyone likes the same things. Not everyone feels capable of doing the same thing. But this list should have on it at least *one* activity that will interest you.

1. *Sports participation.* This can be in such sports as bowling, golfing, swimming, horseback riding, hunting, fishing or hiking. Some people who are interested in this category, share their interest with others by teaching or coaching.

2. *Being an informed spectator.* Certain sports such as baseball, football, basketball or hockey are good choices for watching. You will have a lot more fun, though, if you become an informed spectator.

3. *Collecting as a hobby.* The *what* you collect is not too important. It can be stamps, coins, books, bottles, matchbook covers or ceramic dogs. The important thing is your show of *interest,* your *enthusiasm.*

Collecting will increase your total enjoyment in all areas of your life. You will meet other people who have similar hobbies. You will become a more interesting person.

4. *Artistic expressions and interests.* You don't have to be an expert to enjoy artistic expression and interest. The happy amateur is largely responsible for the continued preservation of all art forms. Painting, sculpture, pottery making, playing a musical instrument, and community theater work are activities in this category. In addition, these activities lead quite naturally into related ones. Museum visits, going to lectures, reading and studying, attending concerts and plays are all a part of your artistic recreations.

5. *Gardening and nature study.* Gardening and nature study can even be done in an apartment. A friend I know has an herb garden in pots which she keeps in her kitchen. She receives as much pleasure from her tiny garden as if she had several acres.

Whatever the size of your garden, you can increase your enjoyment by studying gardening techniques. You may want to join a local garden club.

6. *The art of travel.* This can be either actual travel or armchair travel by means of books and films.

7. *Creative cookery and other home arts.* Gourmet or special-ized cooking can be fun not only for you but for your family and friends as well. Knitting, embroidery and other hand work can be satisfactory hobbies.

8. *Civic interests.* You may want to get involved in local politics or other civic affairs. Charitable organizations are an area in which you can assist. There are volunteers needed in most hospital and homes for the aged. You can make your leisure not only creative but beneficial to the community.

HOW TO CHOOSE YOUR SPECIAL INTEREST

Only *you* can decide how you want to spend your leisure time. Pick a special interest which is suited to *your* capabilities. Pick a special interest which fulfills *your* needs. Pick a special interest which will be lasting. Pick a special interest which has growth possibilities for *you*.

HOW YOUR SPECIAL INTEREST CAN REINFORCE YOUR SENSE OF IDENTITY

A special interest gives an added dimension to your personality. Other people notice this, and as a result you become more interesting as a person to them. You notice it about yourself. Your self-esteem is increased. Your sense of identity is strengthened and reinforced. You become a healthier person and a happier person.

EXTENDING YOUR PERSONALITY AND SPHERE OF INFLUENCE THROUGH LEISURE

You will not only be more popular and happier because of your creative use of your leisure, you will also be more knowledgeable. Do you have trouble making conversation? Do you have difficulty talking to others? You will not have these same problems when you increase your knowledge through your leisure.

Achievement can be a natural accompaniment to leisure. Your self-esteem is raised by knowing what you have *done* or *learned*.

Leisure is a doorway to learning. It can open to new vistas that will change your life.

HOW TO INCREASE YOUR ENJOYMENT OF LIFE THROUGH LEISURE

Empty hours mean an empty life.

Don't blame others if you are bored or frustrated. Don't blame others if you suffer from gloomy Sundays or wasted weekends. You have the power to increase your enjoyment of life. You can choose how you will spend your leisure time.

Check my suggested "Eight Ways To Leisure Hours," and select an activity or a hobby that you would like to try. Don't be afraid to try something new.

Enjoyment can be tripled in your life by the proper use of your leisure time. Why wait to increase that enjoyment? Why wait to collect on your happiness? Start right now!

HOW THE PROPER USE OF YOUR LEISURE HOURS CAN LENGTHEN YOUR LIFE

We all know that there is no real Fountain of Youth. Growing old is a natural process, a universal process. It happens to *all* of us. There is no reason, though, why we can not keep young and alert outlooks all of our lives. The proper use of leisure time will do this for you.

What does your *actual* age matter when you have a personality which is alive and interesting? You will always *seem younger* than you are to people.

In a very practical sense, the proper use of your leisure hours can lengthen your life. If you use your leisure creatively, you are more likely to enjoy good physical health. You will definitely have better emotional health. This combination of factors could *increase* your life span.

A REMINDER

You have *earned* your leisure. It is your best insurance against a wasted life.

Why not really enjoy your life? Increasing your creative use of leisure will increase your happiness.

Don't drive yourself down the path of physical or emotional illness.

Plan your personal program of constructive leisure.

7

How to Profit from Criticism

Criticism is inescapable. No one can avoid being criticized. *You* can not escape criticism. No matter what your position or profession, you will be subject to criticism at some periods of your life.

You can *learn* from criticism. You can *profit* from criticism. You can even learn from criticism which is purely negative in intent.

In this chapter, I am going to show you how you can handle criticism to your best interests. Criticism, when properly understood, can be used to improve your life.

HOW TO UNDERSTAND THE MEANING OF CRITICISM

It is important to understand the *meaning* of criticism. Criticism is not just a simple statement. It is more like the iceberg. Only a part of it is seen. In criticism there is more hidden meaning than is apparent.

By learning to look beyond and below the surface matter of criticism, you can learn its true meaning. Once you have learned this true meaning, you can apply it to your advantage. Understanding the criticism directed at you can *increase* your happiness and success.

THREE IMPORTANT THINGS TO KNOW ABOUT CRITICISM

There are three important things to know about criticism. When you have mastered these three things, you will be in a position to get *positive* results from *any* form of criticism directed at you.

1. The kind of criticism.
2. How to face criticism.
3. How to use criticism.

HOW TO UNDERSTAND THE FOUR BASIC KINDS OF CRITICISM

Criticism can be divided into four basic kinds. Knowing which kind you are dealing with will help you in using it for self-improvement. You do not need to be baffled by criticism. As your first step in handling criticism, decide into which category it falls.

1. *Tactful criticism.* This type of criticism, which is low-keyed and gentle, is helpful. It is easy to accept. You can accept it with the same measure of love with which it is given.

A good teacher uses tactful criticism. A wise parent uses tactful criticism. A person who is kind and considerate offers tactful criticism.

2. *Constructive criticism.* The second kind of criticism does more than criticize. It offers alternative means of action. It provides suggestions and positive responses.

Any leader, whether he be in politics, industry, or a profession, will find that constructive criticism is his best ally in dealing with people.

You can accept it because you know it will contribute to your eventual success.

3. *Blunt criticism.* Criticism given bluntly is difficult to take. It is often harsh, and is usually the result of hasty or poor judgment. Sometimes it is based on a lack of knowledge and understanding.

Don't be thrown by blunt criticism. You can learn to listen and profit from it also. Later in this chapter I will give you some specific suggestions on how to handle blunt criticism.

4. *Hostile criticism.* This sort of criticism, given in a spirit of hostility, is all too frequent. It may be based on spite, jealousy, anger, fear, or other negative emotions. Sometimes it is based on fact, but all too often it is not.

Hostile criticism is the most difficult to face and to accept. But even hostile criticism can be part of your *learning* process. You can turn hostile criticism inside out and into happiness for yourself.

How Margaret N. Used the Tactics of Good Criticism

Margaret N. is one of the best-liked teachers in our local school system. She is well-liked by her students and their parents. She is well-liked by her fellow teachers and other school officials.

She attributes much of her success to her use of criticism in her teaching. She uses *tactful* and *constructive* criticism.

"No teacher of any subject can avoid using criticism," Margaret explained to me, "but, you can use the tactics of good criticism."

Margaret explained that she always thought of two things before she offered any criticism.

"I think about *why* and *how*," she said. "I ask myself *why* am I offering this criticism? Is it because I am tired? Is it because I am feeling irritable? The only valid reason for offering criticism is to help the person. I also ask myself *how* can I offer that criticism so it is useful to the individual?

"A number of years ago I read this about criticism in a book by Arthur Symons. It seemed particularly appropriate for me as a teacher. I copied and still have it in my desk."

Margaret gave me a copy of that quotation. I am going to pass it on to you:

"Criticism is properly the rod of divination: a hazel switch for the discovery of buried treasure, not a birch twig for the castigation of offenders."

Margaret's students learned from her criticism which was tactfully given. She also implanted the seeds of future positive action in her criticism. For example, I overheard her say to a student, "John, your paper on Roman lamps is too short to be acceptable. Also, you did not develop your references properly. However, your section on the social significance of the lamps is very well done. I think if you will take the paper and redo it along those lines, you will have a paper we can *both* be proud to read."

DON'T CRINGE AT CRITICISM

When you receive criticism, don't become depressed or angry. Don't cringe at criticism or become annoyed. It is a sign of emotional immaturity if you can not tolerate being criticized.

Since criticism is so common, you will only make yourself unhappy if you can not respond to it in a positive way.

Criticism is one form of stress, and you must be able to function adequately under it. This is particularly important for persons who are in the public eye. They can not allow themselves to be unduly influenced or upset by criticism.

Sir Winston Churchill had the right attitude when he said, "I do not resent criticism, even when for the sake of emphasis, it parts for the time with reality."

How Roger W. Learned to Face Criticism

"When I first went to work for my uncle in his store, I had a real problem about accepting criticism. I thought he was picking on me whenever he criticized my work. It was my mother who set me right. She pointed out to me that my uncle was very anxious for me to succeed in business. His criticisms were his way of teaching me. She said that his criticism was actually evidence of his interest in me. He had concern about me and my future."

Yes, Roger learned that criticism can also be an expression of *love* when it is concerned with your welfare.

Is there someone in your life who criticizes you or your work? Is there love behind that criticism? Perhaps he is trying to *help* you toward a better, healthier, happier life.

HOW YOU CAN FACE CRITICISM ON THE THREE LEVELS OF IMPACT

Criticism touches you on *three* levels. You must learn how to face criticism on these three levels. They are levels of *impact*, which implies a striking together, or a collision. In this case the forces of criticism are striking at you, and the way in which you respond to the total impact of criticism will determine your emotional good health.

When you can face criticism on the three following levels, you are going to be able to profit from criticism:

1. *Emotional.* It is difficult to avoid having an emotional response—a *negative* emotional response—to criticism. It is on this level of impact that we are most sensitive.

Criticism hurts! It can be as painful as a body injury. It hurts your pride. It hurts your psyche.

Criticism makes you angry. Your negative emotions take over. You become resentful. This is a natural human reaction. But there are dangers in such a reaction. You suffer more than the criticism. Your senses are warped, and you lose your ability to think *clearly*. In a sense, you suffer from a short circuit in your system.

Meet criticism on this level by being *dispassionate*. Keep your degree of excitability *low*.

2. *Logical*. Be *objective*. Look at the criticism from outside. Try to understand the *motivation* behind the criticism. Ask yourself what is the degree of *truth* in this criticism? If it has little truth, dismiss it from your mind and life. If it has truth in it, accept it. Try to see why it is actually justified.

Go from here to the next level of impact.

3. *Practical*. The practical level of impact is the *action* level. This is *where* and *when* you act upon the criticism.

Untrue criticism can be denied. It can be ignored. *True* criticism gives you a chance to improve some facet of your life. Such criticism may act like a detour sign. It tells you that you are going down the wrong road.

How Harlan D. Learned from His Critics

Harlan D. was a successful contractor and civic leader. He had started out in a modest way. His business interests prospered, and he felt secure. He became careless about the quality of work produced by his company.

His business began to fall off. Criticism began to increase.

"At first I tried to ignore the criticism." Harlan told me, "but then it began to make me tense and nervous."

That criticism plus the business losses made Harlan so emotionally upset that he consulted me.

Harlan was an honest man who really did not intend to be dishonest. He tried to ignore the criticism but emotionally and physically it took its toll.

Finally he faced this criticism on all three levels. He admitted that in attempting to ignore the criticism, he had been acting on purely emotional grounds. When he looked at the criticism *objectively* he had to admit to the truth in it.

On the practical level, Harlan improved the quality of work and set new standards for his company. His business affairs improved. His own health improved.

"I almost lost everything," Harlan said, "because I wouldn't face criticism. I learned the truth about myself and my business from my critics."

ARE YOU TOO SENSITIVE TO CRITICISM?

It is possible to be too sensitive to criticism. This extreme sensitivity can cause you needless pain and unnecessary unhappiness.

There are psychological reasons for this sensitivity. Persons who are too sensitive to criticism usually have an *overly severe* superego, that continually tells them that they are no good. It erodes their self-esteem and makes criticism seem more important to their ego.

The overly severe superego comes from parents, teachers, or other authority figures.

An individual with an overly severe superego carries around inside himself a policeman and a censor. He continually listens and watches for words and gestures of criticism. Do *you* have this problem? Do you feel that you are frequently criticized by others? Count up the number of times in the past five days in which you feel you have been subject to criticism. An excessive number may indicate too *much* sensitivity to criticism.

ARE YOU OVERLY RESENTFUL OF CRITICISM?

If you are overly resentful of criticism, you may be suffering from an emotional problem. Individuals with such a problem usually have grandiose ideas and plans. They can not admit to mistakes. They can not accept criticism.

If your opinion of yourself is too high—that is, beyond the bounds of a *realistic* approach to your life—you will have trouble accepting criticism. As long as you think that you are always right, you can not learn from criticism. You can not profit from it.

HOW YOUR SELF-ESTEEM AFFECTS YOUR RESPONSE TO CRITICISM

Either extreme sensitivity or resentment to criticism reflects your degree of *self-esteem,* which, in turn, will affect your response to criticism.

Low self-esteem makes you more vulnerable to criticism. If your appraisal of yourself and your capabilities is low, you will expect to receive criticism from others. When your self-love system is inferior, you feel inferior. You expect criticism; you may even *welcome* it. Criticism reinforces your poor opinion of yourself. A person with low self-esteem is very susceptible to criticism.

When your self-esteem is in harmony with your actual capabilities, you are able to handle criticism.

If your self-esteem is too high and inflated, you *resent* criticism. You may become emotionally disturbed by criticism.

HOW YOU CAN COPE WITH CRITICISM BY BUILDING UP YOUR SELF-ESTEEM

One very good way of learning to cope with criticism is to build up your self-esteem, for as I have said, the person with low self-esteem is very vulnerable to criticism.

Self-esteem is self-respect. It is having a realistic but generally favorable impression of yourself. It is knowing your good and bad qualities and putting the emphasis on the *good* ones. It is a *positive* look at yourself and your life. Self-esteem is *not* self-excuse or false rationalization. It is self-honesty—and it is also a morale booster.

When your self-esteem is high, you can handle criticism. You can look at it *objectively* and learn from it. When you have adequate self-esteem, you are not afraid of criticism.

You can build up your self-esteem. Remember the three hidden *L's* in self-esteem that we talked about in Chapter 3? Using those three qualities, *loved, loving* and *lovable,* you can build self-esteem. You can build self-esteem with the following exercise:

THE FOUR-STEP EXERCISE IN SELF-ESTEEM

This four-step exercise in self-esteem will help you build self-esteem and *maintain* it at the right level. Just as physical exercise will develop your body, this exercise will develop your self-esteem.

You may want to say the exercise aloud, or you may want to write the words down on a piece of paper. Choose the method that best suits you, that suits your purpose.

Do this exercise regularly until you have raised your self-esteem to a high level. After that repeat the exercise whenever it is needed.

1. I am not alone. I have a friend (or friends). My friend respects me. My friend understands me.
2. Someone loves me. He (or she) accepts me as I am.
3. I am a significant person. I have meaning as an individual. I am important to someone.
4. I have a place in the world. I do something useful. I am necessary. I am wanted.

HOW TO DISCOVER AND EXAMINE THE REASONS FOR CRITICISM

It is important to look for and examine the *reasons* behind criticism. This discovery and examination are part of your positive response to and use of criticism.

Try to put yourself in the place of the critic. Why do *you* think the criticism was directed at you? One man I knew who continually criticized other people was actually afraid of being criticized himself. To forestall this, he always took the offensive.

Misunderstanding may be the basis for criticism. You may be responsible for giving the wrong impression about something. You may be an innocent bystander. It does not matter about the situation; it is the misunderstanding which has caused the criticism that is important. Do all that you can to clear up that misunderstanding.

Untrue criticism should be ignored. True criticism should be carefully considered. Sincere criticism has a message for you. Accept the criticism of an honest and sincere critic. *Accept it graciously*—and *learn from it!*

HOW TO HANDLE CRITICISM THAT IS BASED ON SPITE OR JEALOUSY

Criticism that is based on spite or jealousy is very hard to accept because it is *unfair*. It is hostile in intent.

It is best to ignore criticism that is based on spite or jealousy.

Don't stoop to pettiness; don't stoop to the *low* level of your critic. A dignified and restrained silence is your best reply. But at the same time you should try to understand why your critic feels spiteful, jealous or malicious toward you. His attitude may come from a lack of understanding.

There may be times when it will be necessary to refute criticism that is false. This is especially true when it is criticism that verges on the edge of slander that is damaging to your personal or professional life. Do this in a calm way; be unemotional in your actions and words.

FORGIVING IS A GOOD RESPONSE TO CRITICISM

Forgiveness is a very good response to criticism that is unjust or false. What does forgiveness do? It takes away the sting. That criticism becomes less painful and less important in your life. When you can forgive your critic, you are practicing good emotional health. You no longer brood over the injury you have received.

Picture the unfair criticism you have received as being like a balloon. Your forgiveness pricks the balloon and the air rushes out. It is no longer a big object. You have reduced its size—and its *importance.*

WHO IS CRITICIZED?

As I said at the beginning of this chapter, no one is immune from criticism. You must be willing to accept it.

If you hold a position of responsibility, you will be subject to criticism. If you are in politics, you must be prepared for criticism. Any independent decision you make or independent action you take, may cause criticism. You should not expect universal acclaim or popularity.

There is no reason to be too disturbed by a certain amount of criticism. The emotionally mature individual knows that he may rub some people the wrong way. Remember that being criticized doesn't mean not being loved.

HOW TO HANDLE CHAIN REACTION CRITICISM

Chain reaction criticism is sometimes hard to detect—and

frequently difficult to accept. This is the criticism which comes to you *indirectly* because of your close proximity to the critic. It is usually unfair and carping criticism.

Chain reaction criticism bewilders the victim who is unprepared. The suddenness of the criticism is startling.

Marriage and work situations are favorite areas for chain reaction criticism.

We all have a tendency to indulge in this kind of criticism. If we are tense or nervous, it provides a safety valve for our negative emotions. However, while this may *temporarily* relieve one stress, it usually provides another one in its place. Once we have indulged in chain reaction criticism, we usually regret our actions. By that time, damage may have been done in inter-personal relationships.

Chain reaction criticism works this way. Mr. Smith is criticized by his superior at work. He comes home, still seething about the reprimand he has received. The first person he sees is his 16-year-old son who is reading a book. Mr. Smith immediately begins to criticize his son's hair, clothing, and laziness.

Young Smith Junior is upset and angry. He doesn't know what has happened to his father during the day. All he knows is that his father has suddenly jumped on him for doing what he has been doing every day. He is being scolded for being himself when he has been that way for months.

"Why today?" he mutters as he goes to his room and slams the door.

Mrs. Jones works in a store. A particularly demanding customer exhausts her patience. The customer, in criticizing the merchandise, makes Mrs. Jones feel that she is being criticized personally.

After the customer leaves, Mrs. Jones jumps on the stockroom clerk and criticizes his arrangement of stock and handling of material. It is quite easy to suppose that the stockman may go home and criticize some member of his family.

Chain reaction criticism can extend itself far beyond its original starting place. The next time you are criticized, don't pass it on. Let it stop where it is. You wouldn't knowingly pass on a communicable disease. Criticism is just as dangerous. You can not foresee the complications or predict the possible consequences. *Don't be a carrier of criticism.*

HOW TO CONTROL YOUR EMOTIONAL REACTIONS TO CRITICISM

Controlling your emotional reactions to criticism is a mark of maturity. You can learn to *control* those reactions. Adopt an attitude of calmness, of listening to criticism without hysteria or anger.

Be willing to acknowledge criticism that is true. If you have been in the wrong, admit it.

Don't worry about *false* criticism. If your moral standards are high and you maintain them, criticism will not bother you. If your conduct is ethical, your conscience will be clear. You can face criticism, knowing that you are in the right.

CRITICISM IS A TEACHING AND LEARNING PROCESS

Criticism is a way of being *taught*. This is true even when the criticism is offered in a negative way. This is even true of hostile criticism.

We all enjoy being praised. It is only natural to think that we deserve praise for our efforts. This is true. We do need and should have praise. But, the disagreeable and critical things that people say about us can *also* be of use. Those critical remarks can make us *stop* and *think*.

Criticism is one way of learning how to increase your usefulness. It is one way of increasing your happiness.

Don't be too stubborn to learn from criticism.

HOW TO MAKE CRITICISM WORK TO YOUR ADVANTAGE

You can take any kind of criticism and make it work to your advantage. You do this by making criticism a *learning* process. If you find that criticism of your methods or actions is justified, *act* upon that criticism. Change those methods; change your actions.

See sincere criticism as a *guide*—a guide that is trying to show you a better path—a guide that will bring you into greater happiness.

Think of criticism as valuable advice. Criticism may point out a flaw in your actions or life which you have overlooked. Criticism may show up a hidden personal weakness. That weakness may be what is holding back your success and causing you unhappiness.

Treat criticism as an *opportunity*. Treat it as you would a key that can open new doors for you.

A REMINDER

Don't be *afraid of criticism*. *Learn* all that you can from it. *Apply* what you learn.

A clear conscience is your best defense against unfair or false criticism.

Keep your self-esteem at a high level and you will be able to handle *all* forms of criticism.

Criticism can perform a useful function in your life.

8

Why You May Reject the Opposite Sex
and How to Overcome This Tendency

Don't be alarmed if you have emotional problems in your opposite *sex relationships.* You are not unusual. You are *not* doomed to a life of disappointment. You *can* be help**ed.**

In this chapter I am going to show you some common causes of those problems. You will also see possible solutions to those problems, solutions that *you* can apply to your *own* problems.

Your problems with the opposite sex may be caused by early family patterns. They may be problems of sexual identification.

You can learn to become psychologically ready for the opposite sex.

CURRENT LIVING IN OUR MARRIAGE-ORIENTED MODERN CULTURE

This is a marriage-oriented modern culture in which we live. Marriage is presumed to be the goal of each individual. Customs, social mores, legal and religious laws, and taboos all support this point of view. Pick up a copy of any current magazine and the influence of this marriage-oriented culture is clearly seen. The "voice of the turtle" sounds loudly and sometimes clamorously in our land.

It is expected that marriage is the ultimate achievement of life. The success or failure of the marriage is not considered at this time, only the *accomplishment* of marriage.

One result of this marriage-oriented culture is to produce uneasiness and guilt in single people. Too often they are made to feel that they are not normal in some way.

If you are single *by choice,* you do *not* need to feel guilty or unhappy. If you are single but want to be married, you can learn to overcome the emotional problems that may be standing in your way—emotional problems which are affecting your relationships with members of the opposite sex.

THE DILEMMA OF THE SINGLE PERSON

As a single person you may find that you are regarded with suspicion by other people. This will be the case especially if you are in the age bracket of the average marriageable person.

You may be suspected of having abnormal sex interests. You may find yourself spoken of as "maladjusted" or "unfulfilled." If a man, you may be suspected of *impotence.* If a woman, you may be called *frigid.*

An unmarried woman I know was hurt when she overheard herself characterized as "ungiving." In truth, she was a very generous and charitable woman who had not married because of family problems.

More important to you *psychologically* than what other people say or think about your single state, is what *you* think. You may suspect yourself of some of these same things. However, you may be being unfair to yourself. Don't be too willing to accept other people's evaluations. Decide *for yourself* what constitutes your happiness.

If marriage is your answer, work toward that goal. See what is wrong with your responses to the opposite sex. You may be too aggressive. You may be overly timid. Whatever your responses, *they can be changed to bring you happiness.*

THE DANGER OF ACCEPTING THE SINGLE-PERSON STEREOTYPE
AS YOUR IMAGE

There is danger in being willing to accept the single-person stereotype as your personality.

Women especially have a problem if they allow themselves to be brainwashed into accepting such a stock characterization. The old maid has long been a figure of fun and ridicule. But what woman today wants to be part of a joke? Certainly the emotionally mature woman doesn't want to be put in that category.

Single men have a better chance at not being stereotyped. But even they may find themselves characterized as "Mama's boy," "old bachelor," or "sissy."

The implication for both men and women is that they are fussy, rigid, and sexless individuals.

A new stereotype has come into existence in recent years. That is the "single swinger" class. Although it usually refers to men, it can also refer to women. It presents problems of its own as we shall see in the case of David N.

How David N.'s Reputation Was Cheating Him out of His Real Happiness

"I'd really like to settle down," David N. said. "I'm tired of night life. I'm tired of living alone. I'm ready for marriage. I think my friends would all laugh at me though. Even some of the girls don't take me seriously when I say this."

David N. admitted that he had the reputation of being a "swinger" and footloose. He had encouraged that reputation himself by his own actions and words.

"My buddies would really jump on me if I gave up the bright lights for home fires," David explained. "I guess among my friends, I've become sort of a symbol of male freedom."

However, David had decided that a meaningful life was more than just a continuous party. What he needed was to take the next step toward achieving his goal.

I advised David to begin a pattern of alteration in his social life. He was to substitute some other activities for parties. He did not need to cut out his old friends entirely, but he did need to make some new ones—new friends who would have an image of David as a man of *purpose* and *responsibility* rather than as just a single swinger.

David found that he was happier with a social and personal life that *combined* those elements. A few months after making this change in his life style, he met the girl whom he later married. He met her not at one of the parties, but at a political rally.

How Esther Learned to Stop Fooling Herself

"I can't find a husband," Esther complained, "but I'm not the only old maid in the world so I guess I'll get used to it!"

The difficulty was that Esther hadn't gotten used to it. She came to me because she was unhappy. She suffered from indigestion, headaches, and other *psychosomatic* ailments. They were all related to her unhappiness.

Esther was trying to fool herself. She was trying to convince herself to accept a false image. The words "old maid" occurred frequently in her conversation. She admitted that this was her family's conception of her. It was further reinforced by her profession as a teacher, a profession traditionally associated with the unmarried female.

Esther was actually a personable young woman in her early thirties. She was trying to fool herself into behaving like a much older, unattractive woman. She wasn't succeeding.

Through analysis, Esther learned to change her *self-image*. She discarded her old maid concept of herself. She paid no attention to her family's characterization and refused to accept the artificial social limitations of her profession.

When Esther refused to see herself as the old maid, others changed their opinions of her also. Two years after she came for treatment, I received an invitation to Esther's wedding.

SOCIAL AND RECREATIONAL ADJUSTMENTS
OF THE SINGLE PERSON

The single person has to adjust to a social and recreational world which is primarily geared for couples or for family participation. Being excluded from some kinds of recreation or social life makes it difficult for the single person to relate to members of the opposite sex.

Men have always had more social freedom than women. Men have had more choices of recreation. Single men have a social advantage. Single women therefore tend to flock together. They plan group activities. They belong to all-female clubs or organizations.

Are you confining your social or recreational activities to participation with members of your own sex? It may seem better to you now. It may help your loneliness. But it won't help you to be at ease with members of the opposite sex.

You will have to seek out some activities that include both men and women. The well-rounded life is not lived in an isolated one-sex atmosphere.

REJECTION OF THE OPPOSITE SEX CAN OCCUR IN MARRIAGE

Although we have been discussing this problem of rejection chiefly in terms of the *single* man or woman, it is not confined to the unmarried. An unsuccessful or unhappy marriage can be caused by a subconscious or even conscious rejection of the opposite sex. This, however, will be covered in more detail in Chapter 10.

HOW TO KNOW AND REMOVE THE CAUSES
OF AN UNHAPPY MARRIAGE

Keep in mind that rejection of the opposite sex can occur in the single *or* married state. If you are single, this rejection may keep you from marriage. If you are already married, it may result in a separation or divorce. In either case, you are going to be unhappy. You may even become emotionally ill or disturbed.

Whatever your marital state is, look for the *reasons* behind your rejection of the opposite sex. As we discuss the reasons, we will also discuss ways of overcoming them.

SEXUAL IDENTIFICATION PROBLEMS

One reason or cause for rejection of the opposite sex is found in *sexual identification.* In Chapter 5, you learned how identification influences you in choosing your lifework. Sexual identification has an influence on your ability to relate to members of the opposite sex.

Sexual identification patterns are formed during childhood and adolescence. The results of these patterns are seen in adulthood.

Sexual identification problems are concerned with a miscarriage of relationships of the child with the parent of the *same* sex. A boy may find it difficult or impossible to identify with his father. The father may be too domineering—or he may be too weak to assume his rightful position as the father. Growing up, the son of such a father is unable to function effectively as a *strong* male figure.

In a similar way, a young girl needs to have a good identification with her mother. Lack of such an identification means emotional and personality problems in later years.

THE SURROGATE PRINCIPLE

Fortunately for many of us, sexual identification problems can be nullified by *substitute* father or mother figures. This is the "surrogate principle."

A surrogate is one person substituting for another or being put in another person's place. They are acceptable substitutes. They may function more effectively than the original person. Thus, if you have been able to apply the surrogate principle in your life, you will not be suffering from sexual identification problems.

This surrogate principle can be applied if your father or your mother is dead. It can be used if he or she is absent from your life for any reason such as desertion, illness, or divorce. It can compensate for an unsatisfactory parent-child relationship.

A child, especially a boy, needs a hero. When the parent fails in this respect, a substitute, if available, can succeed. In this way, a boy may identify with another male relative, a teacher, or a scoutmaster. A girl may identify with an older sister, an aunt, a teacher, or a neighbor. This process can be done with any person who supplies a stable sense of identification.

REJECTION OF THE OPPOSITE SEX CAUSED BY DISAPPOINTMENT IN THE PARENT OF THE OPPOSITE SEX

You may also reject the opposite sex if you have been disappointed in your parent of the *opposite* sex.

A boy who has a highly unsatisfactory relationship with his mother will usually have difficulty in relating to women as an adult. He may not be able to have a successful marriage. A girl who is disappointed in her father or has no respect for him will carry that feeling into adulthood and project it toward men in general.

This is the principle of *transference*. If you have this problem of disappointment with your parent of the opposite sex, you may have simply *transferred* your emotional reactions toward the parent to another person of the same sex as that parent.

This transference can cause conflict and unhappiness. It can make you *reject* members of the opposite sex. A man will transfer to his girl friend or wife the same attitudes he had toward his mother. A woman will transfer her attitudes toward her father to her boy friend or husband.

If these transference patterns include unfulfilled childhood needs, there will be problems of emotional adjustment. By recognizing habits of *bad transference,* you can keep them from ruining your adult relationships.

Why Kay Felt Compelled to Put Men Down

Kay was, in her own words, getting "jittery" after a ten-year history of broken engagements and unhappy love affairs. She admitted that the problem was caused by her own actions. She would eventually criticize and attack verbally the man with whom she was going. She always managed to find fault with each man and to let him know about it.

"I just seem to feel compelled to put men down," she confessed. "But, I don't understand why."

The "why" turned up during her analysis. Kay had been very fond of her father as a child but in her adolescence she suddenly realized that he was actually a *weak* man. At an age when she needed a strong father image, she saw only a henpecked husband—a father who was not an ideal but an inadequate man.

Kay projected this disappointment to her adult male partners. Through treatment and counseling, she learned to break this habit of *projection* or *transference.*

She later married a man who was close to her ideal of a strong male figure. By this time, however, she had learned to refrain from looking for flaws and weaknesses in men. She had learned to accept a man as an individual and not as a reflection of her father.

How Ron Stopped Acting Like a Demanding Child

Ron felt that he had been discriminated against as a child by his mother. He never felt he had received enough love, attention, and care from his mother.

He did marry, but after marriage, he began to transfer these unsatisfied needs from childhood to his wife. He began to criticize her cooking, her housekeeping and other domestic chores. He insisted that she was not meeting his needs.

"I should never have gotten married," he said, adding, "All women are alike."

In acting like a selfish, immature, demanding child, Ron was abdicating his position as an adult and a husband. Because of his disappointment with his mother, Ron was determined to reject all women.

Like Kay, Ron had to learn not to project the attitudes of the *past* into the relationships of the *present*. He was reminded that just as he no longer played with toys, he also had to put aside his childish *responses*.

When Ron learned to do this, his marriage was saved.

HOW FAMILY PATTERNS CAN BUILD SEXUAL DEFENSE WALLS

Rejection of the opposite sex may be caused by faulty *family sexual attitudes*.

There are two kinds of faulty family sexual attitudes. One is a *passive* response by parents. It is *not doing something*. That "something" is when parents do not display any feelings of sexuality or affection toward each other in front of their children.

I am talking now about gestures and words of affection and love, not overt sexual acts. The child who never sees his parents hug, kiss, exchange affectionate glances, or who never hears words of affection spoken, will have a problem in his own relations with members of the opposite sex.

Coldness and lack of open affection breed coldness. It may produce a *fear* of the opposite sex. This lack of tenderness and affection, as seen by the child, may cause him to think such impulses are *abnormal*. When he feels such impulses of affection within himself, he will be afraid to express them because his parents do not express similar feelings.

The other faulty family sexual attitude is an *active* one in which the parents attempt to *suppress* expressions of love and sexual attitudes as being wicked or sinful. Formerly this attitude was closely associated with religion, and parents were able to enforce their attitudes toward sex by quoting from religious authorities. Today, however, current theology does not subscribe to this kind of attitude. Most modern religious groups take a psychologically sound attitude toward sex and sex practices.

Think back to your childhood. What were the attitudes of your parents toward love, affection, and sexual matters? How have these attitudes influenced *your* attitudes as an adult?

If rejecting the opposite sex is a problem to you, you may still be sitting in the shadow of your parents' attitude toward sex. If your attitude toward the opposite sex is one of *defense* based on *fear*, you may be hiding behind walls your parents build.

Make your own attitudes about affection and sex based on *modern* conditions. Don't be afraid to acknowledge your own love needs.

HOW YOUR PHYSICAL ATTITUDE MAY EXPRESS YOUR HIDDEN SEXUAL FEARS

Did you know that your posture, the way you walk or sit, can indicate your hidden sexual fears? You may not even be aware of what you are doing. Often this physical attitude is in response to carefully repressed feelings.

Try this exercise in self-examination of your physical attitude. Stand in front of a mirror. What do you see? Are you standing up straight? Are you slouching? Do you stoop?

Act natural. Stand as you usually do. Notice how you use your hands. Where do you put your arms? How do you place your feet?

Now sit down in front of the mirror. Notice how you are sitting. Again note your posture, your feet, your arms and hands.

What would you think about a person who stands or sits as you do? What do you think is being expressed? What is being hidden? Think of these in terms of your sexual attitudes.

Here are some guidelines to help you in your self-examination: People who slouch or stoop are trying to conceal their sexuality. Specifically, they may be trying to conceal physical evidences of breasts or sexual organs. A woman who sits with her arms habitually folded against her chest or her legs tightly pressed together is usually indicating a fear of any sexual expression.

Don't attempt to deny your sexuality. Stand up straight. Sit without slouching. Place your arms, hands and feet in graceful positions. *Accept* your body. Have *pride* in your body. *Have pride in yourself.*

CHANGING YOUR CHILDHOOD DEFENSES

During childhood you learn to build up certain defenses, especially sexual defenses. Some of these you learn from your parents. Some you learn from other adults. You may be taught certain defenses by members of your peer group. Your religious training and socioeconomic environment will also play a large part in determining your childhood defenses.

These defenses are necessary since children lack the knowledge and experience to make proper judgments. However, most of these childhood defenses are not valid in adulthood. In fact, they may seriously hamper your emotional development. They may interfere with your ability to accept the opposite sex.

Look at your attitude toward members of the opposite sex. Is it an *adult* attitude? Or are you still behaving like a child?

Since girls are often more strictly raised than boys, women need to guard against keeping childhood defenses. Those defenses may keep women from being relaxed with men; they may keep women from marriage.

Don't be handicapped by outgrown childhood defenses. Trying to build an *adult* relationship between a man and a woman on the emotional level of children is disastrous, as well as foolish. You will not get any further in such a relationship. You will not be happy. It is like trying to ride a kiddy car on the turnpike. It will be a frustrating experience.

THE ROLE OF COMPETITION WITH THE OPPOSITE SEX

In the male-female relationship, competition can be a nullifying factor.

Women are more apt to attempt to compete with men. Men, as a rule, don't bother to compete with women. They simply put women down.

Having been subjugated for so long, women naturally strike back with the weapon of competitiveness. Unfortunately, this does not make for a good relationship between the sexes.

Competition with the opposite sex usually leads to *rejection*. It is difficult to have an affectionate relationship with someone with whom you are competing. Competition and affection produce opposing emotions.

Men feel threatened by this atmosphere of competition. They react by rejecting the woman or women who are attempting to compete with them.

Competition as a stimulus and a motivating force has its place. But its place is *not* in interpersonal relationships.

Why Doris Had Romantic Trouble and What She Did About It

"I can't seem to keep a man romantically interested in me," Doris complained. "We get along fine for a while but then we begin to quarrel and finally drift apart."

Doris was an executive in a large department store. She was attractive and well-dressed. She looked younger than her actual age of 42. But she was lonely and unhappy.

"I know many younger girls envy me," Doris said. "I have a lovely apartment. I can afford the best things. Each year I take a trip. But frankly I would like to have a lasting romantic attachment—perhaps eventually a marriage."

Doris went on to explain that when she had been younger she had been too busy to become romantically involved. Now she had the time but not the same opportunities.

It was easy to see, however, why Doris was having a problem. She was extremely competitive in her attitude toward men. Partly because of her position, she had developed this attitude, and it carried over into her social life. Her attitude had to be changed before she could have a *sustained, meaningful* personal relationship with a member of the opposite sex.

Being an intelligent woman, Doris was able to recognize and admit her mistakes when they were explained to her. In a short time she learned to keep the spirit of competition where it belonged—*in* the business world and *out of* her personal life.

HOW TO OVERCOME OVER-AGGRESSIVENESS
WITH THE OPPOSITE SEX

Over-aggressiveness is caused by feelings of insecurity. It is an expression of *fear*, a kind of whistling in the dark.

If over-aggressiveness with the opposite sex is causing you problems, try this simple test: Look back at your last encounter with a member of the opposite sex. Were there evidences of over-aggressiveness on your part? On a piece of paper, list the form of over-aggressiveness. It may have been verbal. It may have been a gesture or other physical act. *Be honest with yourself.* Now on that same piece of paper write what was the *actual* cause of that over-aggressive act. Again it is important to tell yourself the truth.

A patient who was suffering from tension and anxiety was very aggressive in his personal relations, especially toward women. Through this test he learned to analyze his own behavior. He learned to pinpoint the causes of his over-aggressive actions.

In his case he suffered from two fears. He was afraid of being sexually inadequate, and felt inferior in social situations. Building up his self-esteem helped him to overcome his fears. When his fears were gone, so was his overly aggressive attitude.

HOW TO OVERCOME TIMIDITY AND FEAR WITH THE OPPOSITE SEX

Although wallflowers are a subject for humor, it's not very funny to be one.

Timidity and fear are usually social behavior characteristics that come from childhood. They may be based on experience or on environmental conditioning. They may result from some childhood trauma.

A patient who suffered from excessive timidity with the opposite sex was the victim of a repressed memory from childhood. While in analysis, she remembered an incident which had happened to her when she was about nine years old. At that time a man had exposed himself to her. She was terrified by his actions. This terror was reinforced by her mother to whom she reported the incident. Her mother became hysterical and frightened the child with her stories of the evil ways and nasty habits of men.

This fear had been carried over into adulthood by my patient. With treatment, she learned to overcome this abnormal fear. She could then enjoy a normal and happy relationship with the opposite sex.

Building up your self-esteem will also help you to overcome

timidity and fear. Look at members of the opposite sex as *individuals*, not as "men" or "women."

Some of your timidity may come from *ignorance.* If you are afraid because you are uninformed about sexual matters, read a good sex manual. Or talk things over with your doctor or a professional counselor.

If your timidity is caused by fears of social or conversational inadequacies, you can make up those deficiencies. Through reading you can learn etiquette and other social graces.

By being intellectually alert, you can feel conversationally adequate. One good way of keeping conversationally alive is to read your daily newspaper and at least one weekly news magazine.

Try this before your next social engagement with a member of the opposite sex. It will give you social confidence. You will have a more enjoyable time.

BREAKING THE NEGATIVE COURTSHIP PATTERN

If you have been unsuccessful in courtship over a period of time, you may have adopted a *negative courtship pattern* in your life. You do not need to continue this pattern. You can *break* it.

What constitutes negative courtship? This can be a *narcissistic* attitude on your part. A self-oriented person is not fun to be with and rarely gets a second invitation. Change this by developing an interest in the *other* person. Eliminate "me" and "mine" from your conversation.

Too many men spend their time talking to women about sports, carburetors, and similar topics. Too many women want to talk about home or church matters, children, and minor gossip.

It is important to develop a genuine interest in the other person. It is in this way that areas of mutual interest are discovered and explored.

Negative courtship patterns can also be a subconscious desire to avoid responsibility. A patient admitted that he had developed such patterns because he hadn't wanted to get married. He was often rude to members of the opposite sex. He was selfish and demanding. He lectured and rarely listened. However, when he found a woman he liked and decided to marry, his negative courtship pattern stood in his way. He had to learn to *break* that pattern.

HOW TO BECOME PSYCHOLOGICALLY READY
FOR THE OPPOSITE SEX

It is important that you accept and appreciate the differences between the sexes. When you can appreciate the special qualities of the opposite sex, you are psychologically ready.

You also become psychologically ready by being willing to *extend* your interest away from yourself and toward another individual.

Feeling that these differences between the sexes can enrich your life is also important.

By becoming *psychologically* ready for the opposite sex, you develop the proper *sexual* attitude.

A REMINDER

If you have problems in adjusting to the opposite sex, you can overcome them. If you have a tendency to reject the opposite sex, you can change.

You may have sexual identification problems. You may be still influenced by childhood fears or experiences. You may have hidden sexual fears.

Breaking these negative patterns will help you to become psychologically ready for the opposite sex.

Don't keep your childish attitudes toward the opposite sex. Acting like a mature adult will mean greater happiness for you.

9

How to Determine What Sex Means to You and How to Utilize It Intelligently for a Better Life

James Thurber and E. B. White wrote a book with the title *Is Sex Necessary?* Actually, they were trying to be humorous, but some people have been asking this same question seriously.

Is sex *necessary?* Yes, it is. The problems related to sex come from our inability to properly handle the emotions aroused by this instinctual drive. The *unnecessary* part of sex is the anxiety and tension caused by poor sexual adjustment.

Havelock Ellis wrote, "The omnipresent process of sex, as it is woven into the whole texture of our man's or woman's body, is the pattern of all the process of our life."

In this chapter, I want to show you how you can *use* sex to live a better life. Intelligent understanding of your sexual responses will give you a happier life. It will enable you to have more meaningful personal relationships. It will help you to develop emotional awareness.

HIDDEN MOTIVATIONS IN SEXUAL RELATIONS

Sexual activity is not essential to the survival of the individual, but it does satisfy certain biological, psychological, and emotional needs.

Sexual activity relieves certain tensions which are physiological in origin. Emotional tensions may be either relieved or increased by sexual activity. This will depend upon the circumstances and the motivations.

Many people have hidden motivations in their sexual relations. Their unhappiness and frustration can be directly traced to these hidden motivations.

Sex is sometimes used as a compensation for loneliness. A person who feels left out and depressed sometimes turns to sex in a vain hope of finding happiness and acceptance.

Another hidden motivation in sex is the need for reassurance. Wanting reassurance is not a bad thing. We *all* need some degree of reassurance in our lives. *Lasting* reassurance, however, can not be gained through sex. Reassurance will be discussed in more detail later in this chapter.

Hidden sexual motivations are frequently short cuts which people use to try and find happiness. They are short cuts in *communication,* which fail to achieve their purpose.

SOME QUESTIONS TO ANSWER ABOUT YOUR HIDDEN MOTIVATIONS

Do you have hidden motivations in your sexual life? How meaningful are your personal relationships with members of the opposite sex?

If you are not finding the enjoyment and true happiness you want, ask yourself these questions:

1. What are my *real* motivations?
2. Do I know how to communicate with members of the opposite sex?
3. Am I able to establish a true love relationship with affectional ties?
4. Is it *really* sex I'm after?

Honest answers to those questions will help you to determine the degree of positivism or negativism in your sexual motivations.

HOW SEXUAL PATTERNS REFLECT THE TOTAL PERSONALITY

Your sexual life and sexual patterns reflect your personality—

your *total* personality. You do not become a different person when you act in a sexual role. You still react in the same way as you do in other situations. Your *attitudes* and *responses* remain the same.

Thus, if you are a *passive* person, your sexual patterns will also be ones of *passivity.* If you are basically a *dependent* person, you will look for a sexual relationship in which you continue your role of *dependency.* If you are *aggressive,* you will form *aggressive* sexual patterns. Men who are overly aggressive in their demands often become overly active sexually in a *compulsive* fashion. They develop what we call Don Juan personalities. Women who have similar attitudes frequently become promiscuous in their behavior. Both of these types of behavior will be discussed in this chapter.

HOW YOUR SEXUAL ATTITUDES REFLECT YOUR EMOTIONAL AWARENESS

Sexual drives are instinctual in nature. They are a part of basic human nature. They are a part of the normal make-up of your personality.

Your attitude toward these sexual drives within yourself we call your *sexual attitude.* The kind of sexual attitude you have reflects your emotional awareness.

If your sexual attitude is conditioned by feelings of guilt, fear, or inadequacy, you will suffer from emotional problems. You will suffer from frustration. You will be an unhappy person. You may also run the risk of becoming psychosomatically ill as a result of your faulty sexual attitude.

Good sexual attitudes reflect emotional awareness. By *good,* I mean an acceptance of the nature of the sexual drive and a positive and socially acceptable use of that drive.

Trying to deny the existence of the sexual drive is trying to deny your humanity. It is the *opposite* of emotional awareness: it is emotional blindness.

How Nola's Sexual Attitude Caused Her Headaches

Nola suffered from headaches so severe that they kept her in bed for several days at a time. She finally came for psychiatric help since there seemed to be no *physical* cause for her headaches.

"My doctor has suggested it might be psychosomatic," Nola explained. "I've had new glasses, a complete physical examination, all sorts of tests including X-rays of my skull and encephalograms. I thought that surely I had a brain tumor or a fractured skull, but nothing has ever shown up."

Nola admitted that she had never suffered any head injuries or been in an accident.

"Do you think your headaches are psychosomatic in origin?" I asked her.

"I don't know, Doctor, but I do know that I can't go on suffering like this. Besides, my employer is getting impatient with the many days of sick leave I have had to take. I know he thinks I am malingering but I really am too sick to go to work!"

She *was* actually sick but her headaches, as analysis proved, did come from emotional problems. In Nola's case, it was her sexual attitude that was causing them.

A year before her headaches started, Nola became unofficially engaged to a young man who worked in her office.

"We went together for a year and he wanted me to announce our formal engagement but I just couldn't."

"Why not?"

"I knew he wanted to have the marriage as soon as possible and I just wasn't ready yet."

Now two years later, Nola's headaches were worse and she still wasn't ready for marriage.

"I can't marry anyone when I'm so ill," she explained.

Her original boy friend had stopped seeing her after she told him she couldn't possibly consider marriage for several years.

Analysis revealed that Nola had both a fear of sex and strong feelings of guilt about her own normal sexual drives. In attempting to suppress her natural feelings and emotional awareness, Nola took refuge in headaches. It was a *subconscious negative* response to a faulty sexual attitude.

Eventually Nola was able to change that sexual attitude. She acknowledged the existence of her sexual drive. Getting rid of her fear and guilt made it possible for her to lead a normal life. She no longer had disabling headaches.

Last year Nola married a fine young man whom she met at the home of a friend. Today she is a happy and contented wife.

THE CONFLICT BETWEEN SEXUAL DESIRE AND SOCIETY'S RULES AND HOW TO RESOLVE IT

Nola's trouble was caused by conflict within herself and it was, with treatment, resolved. But conflict may also occur between sexual drive and social standards.

There are two ways of looking at this conflict which is social in its nature. The first is that sexual activity should be *mutually* motivated and mutually agreeable to the participating partners. (My definition, as a psychiatrist, of what is *permissible* is what is mutually agreeable and is consented to by *mature* adults.)

The second way of looking at this possible conflict between sexual desire and society is to be sure that no harm results to anyone in society. If satisfying sexual desire means that someone is going to be hurt or imposed upon, conflict will result. A healthy satisfaction of sexual desire harms no one and is within the limits of our social and cultural structure. It should be noted that by harm, we mean not only *physical* harm but *emotional* harm as well.

THE ROLE OF THE INSTINCTS AND THEIR CONFLICT WITH REALITY

The instincts, of which the sexual drive is one, are centered in the id. As we said in Chaper 1, the id is the pleasure-and destruction-seeking region of the mind. It is *irresponsible;* it is a *delinquent.*

The demands of your id frequently conflict with your external environment. This conflict with reality has to be resolved by your ego. We must learn how to handle these instincts and demands if we want to be happy individuals.

Reality demands that we comply with certain rules and regulations which have been established for the good of society. The id, on the other hand, is very primitive and wants to be satisfied *now.* It is selfish and narcissistic. Your ego, acting as a guardian, keeps these instincts and drives within prescribed limits.

Thus, John Smith seeing Mary Jones walking down the street and being suddenly smitten with her charm, does not rush out and attack her! If his drive is sufficiently demanding, he will find some way in which he can meet her and pursue her in a socially accepted pattern of courtship.

Instinct propels John Smith toward Mary Jones, but a sense of *reality* keeps him from anti-social behavior.

NEUROTIC ILLNESS AND SEXUAL CONFLICT

We have already discussed one case of neurotic illness caused by sexual conflict. Nola's illness was cured when she understood the nature of her sexual conflict.

Individuals who are unable to recognize the fact that they have sexual drives and attempt to repress those drives frequently become ill. They may repress these drives because of guilt, fear or faulty sexual attitudes carried over from childhood.

Do you harbor any feelings of guilt or fear that may be causing you to have sexual conflict with resulting neurotic illnesses? Your negative responses can be caused by a lack of knowledge. They can be caused by childhood trauma. They may be caused by emotional immaturity. But whatever the causes, *you can be helped.*

This repression can cause an anxiety state which may result in such symptoms as insomnia, poor appetite, tremors, irritability, and other signs of tension. These symptoms all indicate a state of conflict between the id and the ego. Or we may say that this is a conflict between the *drives* and the *personality.*

Resolving your sexual conflicts will enable you to live a fully-integrated personal life without the handicap of neurotic illnesses.

CHILDHOOD TRAUMA AND ADULT SEX HABITS

Poor adult sexual attitudes and sex habits are often the result of childhood trauma. A *trauma* is any emotional shock that may result in *permanent* emotional damage. Often it is a violent shock.

Since sex is such an intimate and personal matter, it can, when not properly handled by parents, result in childhood trauma. This trauma affects the life of the adult who may be unable to have a healthy sex attitude.

Parents who tell their children that sex is dirty and sinful are keeping their children from becoming normal happy adults. A father who threatens his children with punishment for their natural curiosity about sexual matters, is handicapping his children for adult marriage. Parents who refuse to give their children adequate and sensible sex education are instilling fear into their children. That fear carried over into adulthood may cause frigidity and impotence.

Confusing repression with morality may lead parents to emphasize *guilt* in connection with sex. Children who are made to feel guilty about sexual feelings find it difficult to easily discard these feelings when they become adults. Marriage, for them, may be an adjustment problem that produces tension and anxiety.

Why Dan Didn't Get Married

"I wish my son, Dan, would get married," a father told me. "He's thirty-five, has a good position, and could support a family. He's perfectly normal but shies away from marriage. I'd like to see him settled down and, frankly, I'd like some grandchildren.

Why hasn't Dan married? His father inadvertently gave the answer in a later discussion about sex education.

"I don't believe in this sex education," he stated firmly. "When I was raising Dan, I told him only what I had to. I saw to it that he didn't do anything he shouldn't do!"

"How did you do that?"

"I told him about the horrors of venereal disease and what happened to your body and mind if you were too interested in sex. I never had any trouble with Dan. He never did anything bad."

Why Frances Had Trouble with Her Marriage

Frances came to me in tears. Her husband, Lew, was talking about a divorce. They had been married only 18 months.

"I don't understand it, Doctor," she sobbed. "I'm a good wife. I like to keep house. I am a good cook. We both enjoy skiing and bowling. Lew admits that he has no complaints about money. We have no in-law problems.

"What about your sex life?" I asked her.

Immediately her face turned red and she became confused, "Oh, that," she said.

It was obvious at once that this was the real trouble with her marriage.

"Do you enjoy being married?" I asked her.

"Oh yes," her face brightened. "I just love to keep house. When I was a little girl, I looked forward to having my own home."

"I meant the sexual side of marriage," I explained.

Frances started to cry again. She was unable to speak.

"Is this the cause of the trouble between you and your husband?"

She nodded.

"Are you afraid of sex?"

Again she nodded and when she regained her composure, we discussed her fears.

"Lew says he loves me, but he doesn't want a friend—he wants a wife. I do love him but every time he wants to make love, I get tense and nervous. I just can't relax. I'm too scared."

Further investigation revealed that her tenseness, inability to relax, and fear all stemmed from one source—her mother.

"My parents never got along," Frances said, "and my mother used to talk to me about how horrible and demanding men were. She said sex was painful and a nuisance. She also told me how she had nearly died when I was born."

Through treatment, Frances learned to overcome her fears. She discarded the ideas that she had received from her mother—ideas that she would become physically and emotionally wrecked by her married sex life—the idea that childbirth was an experience to be avoided at all costs, including the cost of a happy marriage.

As part of her therapy, Frances was encouraged to make friends with young mothers who had happy marriages and enjoyable relationships with their children.

Frances and Lew are still married. Theirs is a happy marriage. Frances is pregnant now with her second child, who is also a planned baby.

THE DANGER OF USING SEX TO FIGHT LONELINESS

You may be mistakenly using sex to fight loneliness. Loneliness is an emotional problem that is all too common in today's world. It is a problem of such concern that I have devoted an entire chapter to this subject (Chapter 13, *How To Overcome Loneliness*).

What is important to say now is that you must look for more practical solutions to your loneliness. Turning to sex is merely turning into a blind alley.

The person who is lonely usually feels rejected by others. He or she suffers from emotional and social insecurity.

If you suffer from loneliness, you may look for fulfillment in sexual relations. What you really want is acceptance by others. What you want is lasting and sincere affection, not merely a physical act. Your needs are psychological and emotional. If you are to have happiness, they must be satisfied on those levels.

HOW SEXUAL CONTACTS ARE USED FOR EMOTIONAL REASSURANCE

As I have already stated at the beginning of this chapter, one of the *hidden motivations* in sexual relations can be the need for *reassurance.* An individual looking for reassurance lacks confidence in himself and in his abilities. The desire to be important is so basic to the human personality that frequently unwise choices are made to achieve the desired end. Wanting to feel needed, this person may seek fulfillment in sex.

Gaining reassurance from achievements, high self-esteem and satisfying personal relationships is a *positive* action. It will give you positive and happy results in your life.

Attempting to get reassurance through sex is a *negative* action. It will give you negative and unhappy results. It will *increase* your feelings of anxiety and tension.

SEXUAL MASOCHISM OF OLDER WOMAN

Older women often mistakenly feel less feminine or think they are less feminine. After menopause, they feel that their days of being sexually attractive are over. This false idea can lead to sexual masochism. *Masochism* is *wilful submission* to pain or indignities. *Sexual masochism* is seeking out and indulging in sexual relations which are personally degrading.

A woman may, in her desperation, become involved with a man who mistreats her. She may even seek out men who are beneath her in cultural and intellectual attainments.

Actually, women *can* and *do* remain feminine all of their lives. They do *not* lose their sexual drives or their desirability.

I am reminded of an anecdote told to me by Princess Marie Bonaparte, the famous psychoanalyst. She was speaking to a group of psychoanalysts and other scientists. At that time she was in her eighties. She was asked when the sexual drive in women begins to wane.

"Ask me later," was her reply.

THE SEXUAL PROFILE OF THE FLIRTATIOUS WOMAN

The flirtatious woman is basically insecure and is trying to reassure herself of her femininity and sexual desirability. She does this by flirting.

Some flirtatious women, however, have other motives in their flirting which is actually hostile in its intent. They feel *inferior* to men. Flirting with men and making romantic conquests makes them feel *superior.*

If you can not resist flirting, you may only be seeking to bolster your own ego. A *meaningful* personal relationship with one person is more satisfying than a series of flirtatious conquests.

THE DON JUAN PERSONALITY

The Don Juan personality is the male counterpart of the flirtatious woman. He is a man who feels sexually inadequate. He may feel inferior and consider himself a failure in his job. Sometimes he feels he has failed as a husband and father.

Romantic conquests are a form of compensation and justification to him. His own image of his masculinity is weak. He attempts to strengthen this image by superimposing on it one of Don Juan, or the great lover.

Actually, he is only hiding behind a paper, or false, concept of his personality. Like the flirtatious woman, the Don Juan man is evading the truth about himself and his feelings.

HOW HOMOSEXUAL FEARS CAN INHIBIT YOUR SEXUAL DEVELOPMENT

False fears about homosexuality can lead both men and women to have poor sexual attitudes. They may avoid sexual matters because they have misinterpreted their own feelings. Misunderstanding and ignorance may cause more emotional problems than any two other factors in your life.

A young man who was in great obvious distress came to me. He blurted out a story of fear of homosexuality. This fear was based on a remark made to him by a cousin who had sneered at him because he was interested not in athletics, but in art.

I pointed out to him that gentleness, a pursuit of the arts, kindness, interest in athletics, and in fact, all personality characteristics have *nothing* to do with determining sexual inclinations. A man who is gentle and kind is merely being a gentleman. He may or may not be interested in athletics or art. Both my patient and his cousin were making assumptions which were based on false ideas and false reasoning.

I would rather reword this section heading to read, "How Homosexual Fears Can Inhibit Your *Social* Development." Many men who have feelings of friendship toward other men fear that such close relationships may be misunderstood.

In your friendship circle there should be a place for friendship with persons of the same sex. This can be an enriching experience for you. The enjoyment of such a relationship is normal. It is an important aspect of your life. It does *not* make you a homosexual.

HOW CONTEMPT AND OTHER HOSTILE FIXATIONS CAN INFLUENCE YOUR SEXUAL LIFE

Your attitude toward members of the opposite sex may contain elements of contempt or hostility. Often these negative attitudes come from childhood experiences.

Contempt or hostility will make it impossible for you to have a happy, meaningful or lasting relationship with a person of the opposite sex. A man who is raised in a family where women are spoken of with contempt, are treated with contempt, or regarded as hostile objects, will grow up and continue to treat women as inferior persons. He may regard them only as sexual objects. His chances of having a happy marriage are very slight.

Hostile attitudes toward a wife are frequently only extensions of hostile attitudes which existed during childhood toward the mother.

Women, too, may develop these hostile attitudes if they have been exposed to hostility toward men. This may then be carried over into their own marital situations.

Frequently a woman who has contempt for men will deliberately seek out a man who is weak in character. When the husband fails, it only serves to reinforce her attitude of contempt.

It is not unusual for a woman raised in a household where the father was an alcholic and an object of family hostility to marry an alcholic. The whole cycle of misery and contempt is repeated in her life and her marriage.

HOW TO TEST FOR HOSTILITY TOWARD MEMBERS
OF THE OPPOSITE SEX

Are there any elements of contempt or hostility in *your* attitude toward members of the opposite sex? Try answering these questions to see what degree of hostility, if any, does exist.

For Men:

1. Do I consider women inferior?
2. Are women primarily of interest to me as sexual objects?
3. Can I communicate with women?
4. What is my attitude toward my mother?
5. Do I get along well with women on a social level?
6. If married, do I have a happy marriage? Do my wife and I have an integrated life in terms of personality adjustment, mutual concerns, and sexual adjustment?

For Women:

1. Do I despise men?
2. Do I look for ways in which I can put men down?
3. What is my attitude toward my father and other male relatives?
4. Have I ever been able to be friends with a man?
5. Do I get along well with men on business and social levels?
6. If married, do I consider my husband an equal partner in our marriage? Are all aspects of my marriage happy and meaningful to me?

Your *honest* answers to these questions should alert you to the presence of any contempt or hostility in your feelings toward the opposite sex. Try to discover the reasons for such feelings—feelings which handicap you in your social relationships—feelings which destroy your chance for a happy marriage.

If these are feelings from attitudes you have inherited, *discard them!* You wouldn't think of dressing the way your parents did, so why carry the burden of *their* faulty attitudes into *your* life?

HOW THE FEAR OF SEXUAL FRIGIDITY OR IMPOTENCE CAN BE OVERCOME.

If the man-woman relationship is a good one, a good sexual relationship will also develop. Mutual concern and understanding can do much to overcome fears of frigidity and impotence.

A defensive attitude may be a barrier to sexual adjustment. Responsiveness in sex, as in other human relations, has much to do with the ultimate degree of happiness achieved.

Frigidity and impotence, *when caused by psychological factors,* can be overcome. Anger and resentment, especially if repressed, can cause frigidity and impotence. It is difficult to face love-making with a partner if you also have feelings of irritation towards that person.

You can overcome your fears of frigidity or impotence by learning to relax. Accept the opposite sex without false attitudes which build barriers between you. Develop patterns of mutual affection and concern.

HOW YOU CAN DEVELOP A SOCIALLY ACCEPTABLE AND EMOTIONALLY REWARDING SEXUAL PROFILE

Your sexual profile, like your personality profile, can be a rewarding one in terms of happiness for you. This can be achieved by developing good, positive attitudes toward members of the opposite sex. Consider them as *different,* but *equal.*

Make consideration part of your sexual attitude.

In areas of sex where you are ignorant, look for knowledge from reputable and professional sources.

Don't let ignorance rob you of sexual happiness.

A REMINDER

Sex has a place in your life, but it should contribute to your happiness. If you are emotionally aware, you will develop good sexual attitudes.

Don't let hidden motivations or repressed hostility ruin your opportunity for good sexual adjustment.

Sex should be a meaningful, personal experience for you. It should be a part of your *total* life picture. It should add to your happiness. It should be an aid to you in your development as a mature, well-adjusted individual.

10

How to Know and Remove the Causes

of an Unhappy Marriage

Perhaps few other social institutions have provoked so much controversy as that of marriage. The pros and cons of marriage have been argued for centuries. Many times the final conclusion given grudgingly by its opponents has been similar to that pronounced by Menander, Greek dramatist of the third century B. C., who wrote, "Marriage, if one will face the truth, is an evil, but a necessary evil." However, just as many people would support these words on marriage written by Martin Luther, "There is no more lovely, friendly and charming relationship, communion or company than a good marriage."

Which statement is true? They both are, depending upon your *attitude* toward marriage. And that attitude is determined by your own marriage. Marriages, good or evil, happy or unhappy, are integrated firmly into our social structure. Much of your personal happiness is decided by your success or failure to make a happy marriage.

In this chapter I will show you what can happen to a marriage to make it an unhappy one. I will also show you how to transform that marriage into a happy one. The final result is not only a happy marriage but a happier *you!*

MARRIAGE STARTS WITH YOU

Despite the poet's contention, marriages are *not* made in

Heaven. They are made on *Earth*. They are made by agreement between two human individuals. Marriage, therefore, starts with you. You have a responsibility to your marriage partner to make it a happy marriage. But that responsibility is also toward *yourself.*

Refusing to do your part in providing the right climate for a happy marriage hurts you. It may cause you more pain and anxiety than it causes your marriage partner.

WHY FAIL IN YOUR MARRIAGE?

If you have an unhappy marriage, you are going to be an unhappy person. You will suffer emotionally. You may also impair your physical health.

Why fail in your marriage? Are you too insistent on your own individuality? Are you insistent on having your own way? It is easier in the long run to work at making your marriage succeed. It pays dividends in happiness and good health.

FUNDAMENTAL NEEDS IN MARRIAGE

In spite of all their interest in careers and equality, most women marry. Most men are ready to give up some measure of their independence for marriage.

Marriage is generally considered to be a desirable goal in life. It is a favored achievement. This is because there are certain fundamental human needs which are satisfied in marriage. These needs may be said not only to be *individual* needs, but also needs of the marriage itself.

Unless the fundamental needs of a marriage are met, that marriage is an unhappy one. It would not, perhaps, be too wrong to say that that marriage is a disaster.

HOW TO KNOW THE SIX FUNDAMENTAL NEEDS OF MARRIAGE

In my practice, I have observed in counseling persons with marital problems that often one or more of these six fundamental needs is *not* being satisfied. Sometimes that need is being wilfully ignored. Other times, it is not being satisfied because one or both partners are simply unaware of that need.

You can learn to know these *six fundamental needs* of marriage by developing emotional awareness. Picture this awareness as an instrument of mental acuity that is attuned to your own personal needs as well as to those of your partner. The fundamental needs of your marriage are a composite of those *two* needs.

THE SIX FUNDAMENTAL NEEDS OF MARRIAGE

Although each marriage may have certain individual needs which are peculiar to that particular union, the six needs listed here are *universal*. This is why I have called them *fundamental*. Another good word to describe their importance would be the term *foundational*.

1. Understanding
2. Companionship
3. Consideration
4. Communication
5 Adequate Emotional Responses
6. Adequate Sexual Responses

UNDERSTANDING IS MORE THAN SAYING YES

One of the prime causes of an unhappy marriage is a lack of understanding. The phrase, "My wife (or my husband) doesn't understand me" has become a traditional and classic joke line. But, in real life, it is not very funny.

A husband complains, "My wife never argues with what I say, but she goes ahead as though she hasn't really listened to me. Last week, I said I wanted to go fishing on Saturday. As usual, she said yes but then on Friday night, she told me that she had invited company from out of town on Saturday so, of course, I couldn't go!"

Another case of saying yes—*without* understanding! The husband in the incident not only enjoyed fishing as a recreation but also *needed* the relaxation.

THE THREE BIG C's IN MARRIAGE

The three big C's are *companionship, consideration,* and *communication.* All three are vital for a happy marriage. The absence of any one of them may be the cause of an unhappy marriage.

Marriage should mean more than two people living under the same roof and sharing certain conveniences. A happy marriage is one in which there is emotional and intellectual companionship. An unhappy marriage is merely a legalized contract permitting sexual union and certain tax advantages between two strangers.

Consideration is the *outward* expression of your understanding and awareness. You are considerate of your spouse when you make the effort to see things through his or her eyes. This practice of empathy, if applied in marriage, would prevent many unhappy or broken marriages.

Consideration is kindness. Consideration is unselfishness exhibited in words and actions.

In our modern technical society, technology has reached new levels of excellence and accomplishment. Yet the fact remains that in an age where communication can be transmitted from a space satellite, a husband and wife may still be unable to communicate with each other. Our personal and emotional achievements in interpersonal relationships often lag far behind our scientific achievements.

Much of the success of a happy marriage can be traced to a willingness and an ability to communicate. Conversely, the opposite is true of an unhappy marriage.

There should be *verbal* exchanges of feelings of love and tenderness. Mark this a regular habit in your marriage. Gestures are also a form of communication. An affectionate pat, hug or kiss is another way of saying, "I love you. You are important to me."

EMOTIONAL AND SEXUAL RESPONSES IN MARRIAGE

Sexual response and emotional responses go together. It is impossible to have true sexual compatibility without emotional compatibility.

Emotional compatibility depends to a large extent upon the emotional health of the individual. If you, as an individual, suffer from tenseness, anxiety, worry, fears and feelings of guilt, you will bring those same feelings to your marriage.

Marriage means different things to different people. You may have an entirely different conception of marriage than your spouse has. Finding the median between your different viewpoints is an indication of your emotional maturity.

Both emotional and sexual responses will be discussed in more detail in later sections of this chapter.

HOW TO DISCOVER YOUR PERSONAL NEEDS IN MARRIAGE

If you are married, take the list of the six fundamental needs as given earlier in this chapter and consider them in the light of your own marriage. It might help you if your write them down on a piece of paper. Check off those which you feel are of *particular* importance to you as a marriage partner.

One woman told me once, "I can manage without as much companionship in my marriage because we have widely diverse interests, but I do need sympathetic understanding and consideration."

Your *personal* needs will vary. They may also vary at certain periods of your life and marriage.

If you have an unhappy marriage, your needs are not being met. This is the time to also ask yourself if your needs are reasonable. Are they the needs of a mature person?

You may be the *primary* cause of your own unhappy marriage.

How Orin Learned to Give Up His Childish Needs

Orin and his wife Betty were on the verge of a divorce. She was in tears as she talked about their unhappy marriage. Orin was sulky.

"I can't seem to do anything right," Betty said "and I don't have time to do everything that he insists I do. This leads to fights and he ends up leaving home. Last month, he was gone an entire weekend!"

"Where did you go?" I asked Orin.

He shrugged, "Nowhere special but someplace where I was treated as an important person!"

As is often the case, a single sentence can furnish the clue to a whole problem. Orin was basically an immature, insecure man who was behaving the same way an immature, insecure child would behave. He needed to be made to feel important.

Further conversations with Betty and Orin showed this to be true. Orin's needs were for almost constant attention. They were childish needs.

"I thought his wanting to be the center of interest was because he had been an only child, and that he would change after our marriage," Betty explained.

Now, after six years, Betty was ready to admit defeat. "I work in an office all day, keep house, and do all the marketing and other shopping. I'm tired most of the time. Orin expects to be waited upon. He also wants me to drop everything and go with him if he decides he wants to go to the movies or for a ride."

Betty was discovering the hard way that instead of having no children, she had *one* child—32 year old Orin. When he didn't get his way or felt disappointed in Betty, Orin took a typically childish way out. He *ran away.*

Orin's parents were dead or he probably would have gone home. Instead, he went to a motel where his money purchased the service and deference he needed for his sense of importance.

It was not easy for Orin to learn to give up his childish needs. In time, and after treatment, Orin literally grew up. He became an *adult* partner in his own marriage. He learned to share some of the responsibilities of home life. Betty and he planned together their recreational times. The next time Orin went to a motel, he took Betty with him.

"We both had a good time," he reported. "It was restful and fun."

Betty's smiling face corroborated his statements.

Orin had discovered the cause of his unhappy marriage— himself—and had been able to change that cause.

HOW TO HAVE GOOD EMOTIONAL RESPONSE IN MARRIAGE

Emotional maturity is essential for a good emotional response in marriage. That maturity has to be based on a high level of self-esteem in every partner. This self-esteem leads quite naturally to a feeling of security.

Each marriage partner must trust the other. Each marriage partner must feel secure and loved. The marriage partner who is emotionally mature can do this and feel at ease in his or her marriage.

Involvement is a part of your emotional response to marriage. Involvement is *sharing.* Involvement is *concern.* Involvement means *tactful responses.* Unless both partners are *totally* involved, the marriage will be an unhappy and unsuccessful one.

Humor is a part of your emotional response to marriage. A sense of humor and the ability to share laughter are essential to a happy marriage.

Free expression is another part of your emotional response to marriage. Both you and your partner should have the freedom to express your personalities to each other and expect to receive sympathetic understanding.

TRANSFERENCE AND MARRIAGE PROBLEMS

Transference is another form of emotional response to marriage.

As we learned in Chapter 5, transference is the transfer of childhood emotions to people other than the original recipients. It is the inappropriate appearance of childhood emotions in adult situations. This often results in conflict, which produces tension and anxiety. The final result is unhappiness.

Transference is frequently the cause for unhappy marriages. Transference phenomena in marital problems occur when one partner is experiencing the other partner as someone else. A husband's attitude toward his mother may be summarily transferred to his wife. A wife's attitude toward her father may be transferred to her attitude toward her husband.

This can be very evident when the feelings of a partner are *inappropriate* to the situation. This is usually seen in anger where the degree of rage is inconsistent with the supposed misdeed. Transference is responsible for most of the unhappy marriages. The inability of a marriage partner to see his or her spouse as they are leads to trouble.

Incidentally transference does *not* depend upon whether or not the parents are dead or alive. Neither does it depend upon the closeness or compatibility of the relationship with the parents.

Transference is usually an unrecognized cause of marital problems until it is brought out in the open.

You can test your own marriage for transference. Ask yourself these questions:

1. Are my feelings too intense for the response that should be called for?
2. Do I see my spouse as he or she is or do I see my spouse as someone else?
3. How do other people see my marriage partner? Am I the only one to see him or her as I do?
4. Could I possibly be wrong in my mental picture of my husband or wife?
5. Who is the person I am trying to superimpose on my spouse?

The Case of Misplaced Anger

"My wife is really a good wife but she gets terribly angry if I break anything," Paul said. "Last week I accidently dropped a glass and I thought she'd kill me. It wasn't an expensive glass or an antique. As a matter of fact, it was a glass I got at the gas station with ten gallons of gas."

Paul was puzzled by these inappropriate angry responses of his wife. "One time she wouldn't speak to me for several days when I dropped a flower pot and broke it."

Since Paul reported that his wife's disposition was reasonably amiable in all other areas, transference was suspected as the villain. Paul's wife later confirmed this theory.

"I just get wild when anything is broken." she admitted. "I get so furious I can't talk sometimes. I have a great desire to punish the person who did the breaking even when I know it's an accident."

Further inquiry brought out the fact that her father, a stern and sadistic man, had always punished her by breaking a favorite toy or possession.

"Once it was my favorite doll," she recalled, "and another time when he thought I had told him a lie, he took a hammer and smashed my doll dishes. I was late getting home from a date when I was 17 and he took an axe to my radio."

She admitted that she had been angry at this kind of treatment but had never shown it. "I was afraid of him," she said.

This anger had been transferred to her husband. When he broke something, she immediately flew into a rage which was really directed toward her father for past incidents. Once she had learned the *real* reason for her outbreaks of violence, she was able to handle her feelings within the bounds of normal reactions.

This case of misplaced anger ended successfully with a better-adjusted wife and a resulting happier marriage.

AN EMOTIONAL RESPONSE QUESTIONNAIRE

What are your emotional responses to *your* marriage. Are they contributing to a happy marriage? Or are they a possible cause of an unhappy marriage.

Honest and thoughtful answers to these questions will help you in evaluating your emotional responses to your marriage.

1. Do I like myself?
2. Is my self-esteem high?
3. How emotionally mature do I act?
4. Do I trust my marriage partner?
5. Do I feel secure in my marriage?
6. Do I feel loved?
7. Am I involved in my marriage?
8. Do I show concern toward my spouse?
9. Am I willing to share in the responsibilities of my marriage?
10. Do I use tact in my marriage relationship?
11. How much laughter is there in my marriage?
12. Is this *shared* laughter and humor?
13. Do I repress my true feelings and conceal them from my wife or husband?
14. Do I encourage my wife or husband to freely express feelings, ideas, and attitudes without fear of anger or ridicule from me?
15. Is sympathetic understanding an ingredient in my marriage?

HOW TO USE SEX TO BUILD A HAPPY MARRIAGE

The *true* significance of sex in marriage is its function as a further expression of mutual trust and love. It is a form of subtle and important communication between two very different human individuals. It is the highest form of reassurance that can be given in a marriage relationship.

Sex can only be used to build a happy marriage when it is given as a joyful gift. Happiness is gone when sex is demanded by either partner, or used as a weapon by husband or wife.

There are two important things to remember about the use of sex in your happy marriage pattern. One is that ignorance is *not* bliss; it can be misery. The happiest couple is the couple that have informed themselves on sexual matters. If you feel that your lack of knowledge may be keeping you or your partner from achieving satisfaction, *seek help.* Your doctor, a trained counselor, or a well-written authorative marriage manual can assist you in your sexual adjustment questions or problems.

Two, don't let fatigue make it impossible for you to have a satisfactory married sex life. Allow yourselves time to *relax* and *rest.*

An atmosphere of love—expressed through the many facets of married life, including sex—will almost certainly guarantee you a happy marriage.

HOW TO SHARE RESPONSIBILITIES IN MARRIAGE

Throughout this chapter I have been using the term "marriage partner." This is deliberate. Marriage *is* a partnership. A happy marriage is a marriage of joint responsibilities. It is a sharing. While each partner may have certain prime areas for which he is specifically responsible both partners should take an interest in *all* areas.

A wife, if she stays at home, should know that she can discuss her problems with her husband. By the same reasoning, she must be a willing and knowledgeable listener to her husband when he talks about his work.

A husband should be aware of how and why his household is run and not take it for granted. He should be willing and able to help his wife if she needs help. This is particularly true in marriages where the wife works outside the home.

But more than work needs to be a matter of joint responsibility. Money and financial decisions can contribute to the success or failure of a marriage depending on how they are handled. Working together for a common goal will help to eliminate problems caused by finances. It can be a house, an automobile, a vacation, or a new set of furniture.

Mutual agreement about other things will also contribute to a happy marriage. Since marriage partners are not automatons who always think alike but individuals with often divergent views, *compromise* is essential.

Give and take with a mutual acceptance of responsibility is a good rule for a happy marriage.

HOW TO COPE WITH OUTSIDERS IN YOUR MARRIAGE

Once you are married, anyone *outside* that magic circle of two is automatically an *outsider.* Your family, close friends, even your children are technically outsiders.

Unfortunately, many people don't want to accept that premise. Sometimes the fault is caused by one of the marriage partners who insists on placing an outsider on an equal footing in the marriage relationship.

"May has been a friend of my wife's since kindergarden," one husband complained, "and that's fine, but I didn't marry May too. My wife tells her everything first and confides in her instead of in me. I resent May and her position in my marriage."

"My husband won't decide on a thing unless he first talks it over with his parents. I think that now that he has married, he should make a decision *after* he has talked things over with me!"

"After the children came, my wife seemed to put them first. I feel left out of her life."

These are all typical statements by unhappy married partners who feel that they have been shortchanged in their marriages.

If your marriage is unhappy, could an outsider be the cause? Perhaps you need to redefine the limits of that magic circle for two. Remember—it was designed to hold only *two* with comfort and ease. Trying to crowd others in will ruin your chances for happiness.

HOW TO STRIKE A BALANCE BETWEEN OUTSIDE ACTIVITIES
AND HOME INTERESTS

People in love who marry usually can not believe that their private world will ever be impinged upon by outside activities or forces. While this is an understandable romantic thought, the truth is that life *does* go on. Not only do their lives go on, but so does the busy life of the world around them.

All too soon, the phrase "At last we are alone!" is changed to "You don't love me any more!"

An inability to accept outside interests is a sign of emotional immaturity. So is an inability to properly balance outside activities with home interests. All work and no play not only makes *Jack* dull but it makes Jack's *marriage* dull. It also makes Jill's life unhappy.

Too much outside activity, whether it is work or fun, is only a form of running away from domestic responsibilities. It is basically a childish reaction to adult life. It can wreck a marriage. The husband who is an avid golfer and spends every free moment at this sport is cheating his marriage. The woman who plays bridge and neglects her family and housework is also cheating. But so is the man who spends long hours away from home because he is involved in lodge or civic club activities. So is the woman who is overly busy in volunteer or church work. All of these people are evading their prime responsibilities for reasons that may vary.

"My husband just sits in front of the TV every night. I might as well not be home."

"My wife is only interested in the children."

"My wife is such a fussy housekeeper, she's glad to have me out of the way."

"My husband is tired most of the time so I go without him."

It is just as bad to *overemphasize* home activities over outside ones. The man who spends all of his time in his basement workshop should be building his marriage instead of more bookcases. A happy marriage is one in which there is a careful and thoughtful balance between interests, between the two worlds.

What about *your* marriage? Have you been able to strike a proper balance between outside activities and home interests? If you haven't, it may be the cause of unhappiness in your marriage.

MAKING AN ACTIVITIES CHECK LIST

Making an activities checklist is a way of determining whether or not you have achieved the proper activities balance in your marriage:

> On a piece of paper
> 1. Write down all of your activities for the past week, or all of those for an average week. *Include everything.*
> 2. Circle in *red* those activities which you have done *outside the home.*
> 3. Circle in *blue* those activities you have done *at home.*
> 4. Add up your two sets of circles. How do they compare?
> 5. Estimate the number of hours involved in each of the two sets. How do these figures compare?
> 6. Place an *X* on the circles where that activity has also been one you shared with your marriage partner or some other member of your family.
> 7. Add up your *X*'s. How many hours of your time do they account for in your schedule?

This activities checklist will show you if you need to make some changes in your activities pattern.

HOW TO BLEND TWO DIVERSE PERSONALITIES IN MARRIAGE

Marriage brings together two diverse personalities. No matter how much you have in common with your marriage partner, you are still distinct individuals.

Differences can cause conflict, and can be a cause of an unhappy marriage. Resolving those differences does not mean giving them up; it means *adjusting* them. It means compromise and sharing.

"I like football and my wife prefers the symphony," one happily married man told me. "We agreed early in our marriage that we would each show an interest in our individual activities. We have season tickets to both the football games and the symphony. I've learned a lot about music and my wife can talk to me about sports.

Another couple solved their differences in taste this way:

"My husband likes what he calls 'plain cooking' and he prefers to eat at home, but I enjoy fancy food and eating out. We worked this out by going out to a nice restaurant two or three times a month. The rest of the time I cook his favorite foods at home."

Don't be upset by the differences between your marriage partner and yourself. *Enjoy them.* Sharing your individuality with each other will only add to your own personalities. You won't lose a thing—but you will *gain* a great deal.

HOW A HAPPY MARRIAGE CAN SATISFY YOUR PSYCHIC NEEDS

A happy marriage gives you a chance to be loved. More important to your development as a well-integrated and mature personality, it gives you a chance to *love.*

Your psychic needs to show and receive affection, concern, and interest can all be fulfilled through a happy marriage. Knowing that you are important to and needed by another individual will raise your *self-esteem.*

A REMINDER

A happy marriage isn't an accident; it is planned.

Don't be afraid to be considerate toward your marriage partner. Don't be too proud to communicate.

Be willing to share the inevitable work of maintaining a home. Be also willing to share on an emotional level.

A happy marriage means more creative, more productive lives for you and your marriage partner.

11

How to Give the Best of Yourself

to Your Family

Despite many innovations in the twentieth-century social order, the *family* has remained as an important unit of our social structure. It will, no doubt, continue to be important.

The family unit is the basic or keystone unit in our culture. This has been the case since the beginning of human interrelationship. The early living patterns were established as family patterns.

Mencius, the ancient Chinese philosopher, summed it up in this fashion: "The root of the kingdom is in the state. The root of the state is in the family. The root of the family is in the person of its head."

In this chapter, I want to show you how you can *get* more happiness out of your family relationship. I want to help you to *give* more happiness to your family. You can learn how to give your *best* to your family.

THE COMPLETE FAMILY

Traditionally, the complete family consists of the father, the mother, and the children. We see this in the play of children when they play house. For them, the family is a closed circle.

Often, particularly in past years, the family also contained many peripheral persons. These were grandparents, aunts, uncles, and other family relations. In addition, there were often servants who had family status. Now the complete family is a small group usually consisting of one or two parents and school-age children.

Technology has ruptured the family circle. But, because of these very demands of our technical society, *good* family relationships are important. They are important for our personal development and happiness. Living successfully with *yourself* is also living successfully with your *family.*

CONFLICT IN THE FAMILY GROUP

Conflict can readily occur in any close-knit group unless preventive measures are taken. Conflict in the family group can occur with frightening regularity. It can have dangerous results. It can have permanent disastrous consequences that weaken the family group.

Not only does conflict inflict damage on the family as a living unit, but it also damages each person in that family group. You lose two ways when there is conflict in your family. You lose as an individual, and you lose as a family member.

SEVEN COMMON EXPRESSIONS OF CONFLICT IN FAMILY LIVING

There are seven common expressions of conflict in family living. They range from the most obvious to the more subtle.

1. *Quarreling.* Quarreling is the most readily recognized form of conflict. Quarreling may occur between only certain members of a family, as between husband and wife or between mother and daughter. Quarreling may also be an all-family trait. Quarreling contains one or more of the other expressions of conflict.

2. *Shouting.* Shouting may be a part of quarreling or exist as an independent action. Whole families sometimes seem never to be able to employ normal conversational tones. They shout, they scream, and they yell at each other.

3. *Bickering.* Bickering differs from quarreling in that it is low-keyed and usually constant. In its constant action, it becomes extremely abrasive.

4. *Sulkiness.* Sulkiness is often accompanied by silence. And that silence is as wearing in its way as is shouting. It holds an explosive

force that threatens at any time to totally disrupt the family situation.

5. *Disloyalty.* Because of its intimate nature, the family needs and should receive loyalty from its individual members. Disloyalty is always a sign of conflict.

6. *Cruelty.* Cruelty in any form is an overt expression of conflict. It can be physical mistreatment, but it also can be a form of mental or emotional cruelty. Lack of consideration is basically a form of cruelty. Like cruelty, it can harm both physically and emotionally.

7. *Indifference.* Indifference is a conflict weapon in the family circle. It is a deliberate choice by the user. He or she knows that indifference hurts—and *wants* it to hurt.

These seven expressions of conflict show up in words, in actions, and in the home atmosphere.

HOW TO TEST YOUR FAMILY CONFLICT LEVEL

What is your family conflict level? If it is too high, you are cheating yourself and your family out of happiness.

Test your family conflict level in this way: Write on a piece of paper the seven common expressions of conflict in family living. Write them in a column. Across the top of your sheet of paper write these words: ALWAYS, FREQUENTLY, OCCASIONALLY, RARELY, and NEVER.

When you have finished, your paper should look like this:

ALWAYS	FREQUENTLY	OCCASIONALLY	RARELY	NEVER

Quarreling
Shouting
Bickering
Sulkiness
Disloyalty
Cruelty
Indifference

Now, check your family against this list. Be *honest* about your family conflict attitudes. Put a check mark in the appropriate column.

All families will quarrel occasionally, or have other conflict situations develop. Don't worry about *normal* amounts of conflict in your family. This is quite natural. However, *too many* checkmarks in the ALWAYS or the FREQUENTLY column should be an indication to you that you need to change some family patterns.

HOW YOU CAN CHANGE YOUR FAMILY CONFLICT LEVEL

If you find that your family conflict level is too high, you can change it. You can lower it to an acceptable normal level.

One way is by understanding the reasons *behind* your family conflicts. In this chapter you will have helps and suggestions that will enable you to look below the surface in your family relationships.

Another way is by learning to substitute the *positive* responses of consideration, tact, loyalty, kindness, intelligent understanding and acceptance, for the existing *negative* ones. It is these negative responses which provide the climate for conflict in your family.

You give your best to your family when you respond positively to them. You also in this way encourage the formation of positive attitudes and responses from other family members.

Giving your best can become a family habit.

HOW CHILDHOOD TRAINING AND TRAUMAS AFFECT
ADULT FAMILY ATTITUDES

As adults we reflect our childhood training and all of our childhood experiences. Both good and bad experiences are remembered and influence our adult behavior, thoughts, and attitudes.

One of the most common results of the adult-childhood link is the *repetition compulsion,* an unconscious attitude which compels us to repeat things that happened to us in childhood. Or, it can be expressed this way—repetition compulsion is a mental process which causes us to repeat *actively* as adults what we experienced *passively* as children.

Any traumatic experience you may have had with your parents

becomes incorporated into your superego. It becomes part of your unconscious. Now, as an adult, you adopt that same attitude and behave in the same manner your parents did. *Consciously*, you may wish for a different response, but *unconsciously* you feel compelled to repeat the parental response.

All youngsters have a period in which they announce: "When I grow up I am going to treat my children in a different way!" Then they grow up, become parents, and raise their children in the same way in which *they* were raised.

This is a negative identification with the parents. It does not produce family harmony or happiness. It continues to perpetuate a lack of understanding between parents and children.

How Mrs. Jones Broke the Habit of Repetition Compulsion

"I'm upset and nervous all the time," explained Mrs. Jones. "I don't get along with my children. Our home life is miserable and I feel it is my fault."

Mrs. Jones had a mental picture of the mother she *wanted* to be to her children — warm, loving, kind, and understanding. Her inability to be that kind of a personality was making her tense and depressed.

"I find that I am always yelling at the children," she confessed, "and I use abusive language toward them. I really love them but I seem compelled to mistreat them verbally. I'm afraid that they will grow up to hate me. Already I can see that the older children prefer to stay away from home as much as they can."

During therapy, the fact was brought out that Mrs. Jones' mother had always yelled at *her*. And although Mrs. Jones had, as a young girl, resolved that she would never do this to her own children, she had. Mrs. Jones admitted that she was particularly hard on her daughter just as her own mother had singled *her* out for abuse.

Therapy helped Mrs. Jones to break the habit of repetition compulsion. It took time, but she learned to speak softly rather than yell. She learned to choose her words and express herself more temperately.

"The children actually pay more attention to me," she reported. "Our home is a pleasant place now and we are doing more things together as a family."

EMOTIONAL INTERDEPENDENCE IN THE FAMILY

Do not be afraid of being dependent upon other family members or of having them be dependent upon you. This is normal family living. The family member who stresses his independence is not acting in an acceptable way. Often, he or she, regardless of age or family position, may be emotionally upset or sick.

Family interdependence is a good thing. It is a *sharing* process built up of consideration, loyalty, concern, and love. *Emotional interdependence* is when family members depend upon each other for love and warmth, as well as for basic physical needs.

A successful and happy measure of family interdependence makes possible emotional and mature forms of adjustment to persons *outside of the family circle.*

IDENTITY PROBLEMS AND FAMILY ADJUSTMENT

Identity problems sometimes occur because family members are also individuals. Mothers are not just mothers; they are also women with certain basic female drives and desires. Fathers are also men with male identities. Children, as they grow into adolescence and adulthood, develop their own sexual identities.

It is necessary to be able to keep your personal identity and your family identity compatible. Some situations can produce trouble if they are not properly handled. These are identity crisis situations.

One of these situations may occur at the time of the birth of a male child. A father, even though joyful at this news, may feel a kind of jealousy. A son is a threat to his own male position in the family. This same situation of rivalry may become even more a problem when the son becomes an adolescent.

There is often a keen sense of competition between fathers and sons. This is more often the case where a father's sense of masculinity is not strong. His son, by contrast, has that sureness of masculinity which is frequently a part of adolescence. Feeling his son to be a threat, the father may become unkind or even abusive toward his wife.

Mothers tend to have identity crises when their children go to school or become old enough to leave home. They suffer from a sense of loss and from separation anxiety. Although parents, particularly mothers, know that one of their functions is to prepare children for the outside world, they still may find it hard to accept this fact.

Theory and *training* go very well, but *reality* and *practice* are more difficult!

HOW TO COPE WITH IDENTITY PROBLEMS

It is not possible to eliminate identity problems, but it is possible to *cope* with them. That is family adjustment working at its best.

Take your various identities. Picture them as each drawn on a transparent sheet. You need to overlay the various sheets so they have a kind of final and harmonious unity. Father, husband, and male identities have to fit together and not compete with each other. So do the mother, wife, and female figures need to work well as a single unit—but with three possible viewpoints.

You can cope with identity problems by self-understanding. Understand your role as a parent. Understand and accept its responsibilities and its limitations. In a similar way, understand your role as a marriage partner.

Develop and keep high your self-esteem and your understanding of yourself as a unique and valuable individual. Accept yourself in relation to the others in your family circle.

HOW SELF-DISCIPLINE CAN MAKE A SUCCESSFUL FAMILY RELATIONSHIP

Although much is written about discipline in the family and its importance and proper use, self-discipline is just as important. A successful family relationship demands self-discipline from all members—not just from a few. The old days of the Victorian ideal of the stern but sometimes unreasonable parent have passed. *In the happy family there are no tyrants!*

Using self-discipline means that you learn to block those negative emotions which lead to outbursts of irritation, anger, or carping behavior. All of these things destroy the family relationship.

Children or marriage partners are frequently shocked to find themselves exposed to inappropriate anger—anger which is out of proportion to the supposed cause or offense. A mother or father who "blows up" at some trivial offense is displaying inappropriate anger. This anger is often the result of transference.

Transference, as we learned in earlier chapters, is the transfer of emotions to people other than the original ones for whom they are intended.

Mr. T. has a disagreement with his boss. He is seething when he comes home. He has not been able to discharge his feelings because he does not want to jeopardize his job, which he needs. As he pulls into the driveway, he sees that his son's bicycle is in the way. Slamming on the brakes, he storms into the house and screams at his son. He not only yells about the present offense, but he also reminds the boy of other misdeeds.

Mr. T. has successfully transferred his anger at his boss to another object—his son. He has, however, acted unsuccessfully as a father and as an adult. As a result of his inappropriate anger, his son is bewildered and resentful. Other family members are tense. The home atmosphere is filled with anxiety.

A mother who finds that her cooking has failed may turn and slap her child who is unlucky enough to make a noise at the wrong time.

Inappropriate anger and other problems of negative reactions can be controlled through habits of self-discipline. Self-discipline comes through insight. You must learn to understand yourself and your motivation. You must learn to examine and understand your emotional responses.

How Hugh Learned Self-Discipline

"It's my home so I feel I can act just as I want to!" Hugh insisted. "After all, if your family can't put up with you, why have a family?"

But Hugh's family was finding it more and more difficult to put up with him. His wife was considering a divorce. His children were alienated from him.

"Acting just as I want to" meant being cross, mean, inconsiderate, and demanding. A hard-working businessman, Hugh behaved at home in a way he never would have tolerated among his business associates. His refusal to extend the limits of consideration, kindness, and thoughtfulness to his home was costing him dearly.

Hugh finally did learn the difference between self-*indulgence* and self-*discipline*. He began to see himself as his family saw him. It was not an attractive picture!

He admitted that it was unfair to his family to expect them to put up with his tantrums and poor manners. He realized that he could not win and keep his family's love and respect by acting like a spoiled child. Hugh saved his marriage and regained the affection of his wife and children by using self-discipline.

Do you, like Hugh, have a self-discipline problem in *your* life? Can you, like Hugh, make the effort to apply self-discipline to *your* life?

You *can*—and you should start *now!*

HOW CONSIDERATION CAN ADD FLAVOR TO FAMILY HARMONY

Just as seasoning adds flavor to food, consideration is that added ingredient that adds flavor to family harmony. Putting consideration into your family living means taking out irritation and conquering the habit of getting annoyed by petty or trivial concerns. Being considerate means applying the principle of the golden rule to your family interrelationships and using the principle of empathy in living and working with your family.

Empathy is using your imagination to put yourself in another's place. It is a way of enlarging your powers of sympathetic understanding. It is easier to get along with other people when you have some conception of what they, themselves, are feeling and experiencing.

"Our marriage and family life have been happy and harmonious because of mutual consideration," explained Mrs. V. "My husband and I resolved that we would not allow habits of rudeness, unconcern, or thoughtlessness to become a part of our family habits."

Consideration is that vital margin between family happiness and family unhappiness. If you have a discord problem within your family, try solving it with a liberal application of consideration.

DON'T IMPOSE ON YOUR FAMILY

You are not giving of your best when you impose on your family. You are really giving of your *worst!*

None of us like to be imposed upon. Imposition irritates us. Because we are aware of the feelings that can be aroused, we usually hesitate to impose on other people. Often there is an exception to this rule; persons who would *never* impose upon friends or acquaintances have no hesitation in imposing upon their family.

Do you employ a double standard of imposition? Are you as considerate of your family members, their plans and wishes as you are of other people that you know?

Do you treat your family in a way you would *never* treat your business associates?

If you have doubts about your degree of imposition, try the Imposition Test given below.

IMPOSITION TEST

Take a look at your relationship with your family and determine the degree of imposition involved in that relationship.

Ask yourself these questions; check the appropriate column.

	ALWAYS	OCCASIONALLY	NEVER
1. Am I late for meals?			
2. Am I a fussy eater?			
3. Do I demand special attention from my family?			
4. Am I neat or do I expect someone else to pick up after me?			
5. Do I keep up my personal appearance at home?			
6. When family plans are made do I consider them in my own plans, or do I ignore them if I prefer to do something else?			

<u>ALWAYS</u>   <u>OCCASIONALLY</u>   <u>NEVER</u>

7. Do I try to enforce my views, desires, and plans on the rest of the family?

8. Do I expect my family to put up with my moods?

9. Do I insist that my family accept my displays of anger, irritation, or just plain bad manners?

10. Do I consistently demand more from my family than I am willing to give them?

USING THE PRINCIPLES OF FAMILY THERAPY AT HOME

It is possible—and desirable—to use the principles of therapy at home. Family therapy is a way of solving problems as they occur. It is also a way of preventing many problems. Problems, disagreements, and tensions all place strains upon the family. If you can avoid the unnecessary strains by using family therapy, you will have a happier family and a stronger family unit.

Don't be afraid to face your family problems. Hiding them does not make them go away. In fact, they usually become larger and more difficult to handle.

Confrontation is essential to the practice of effective family therapy. Confrontation is a face-to-face process by which troublesome things are brought out into the open.

Picture confrontation as a circle in which the family meets. Within that circle there must also be smaller circles of individual self-confrontation.

Successful group confrontation requires a measure of successful individual self-confrontation. Family awareness comes out of the smaller units of self-awareness. Confrontation in family therapy is a way of putting things in proper perspective. It is group estimation of group problems.

"But we don't have group problems!" a patient once objected. "We have individual problems."

I pointed out to him that when individual problems disturb the harmony of the family or group, then they become group problems. They require family therapy and group action.

The objective of family therapy is to *change* those things which are having an adverse effect upon family happiness.

Family therapy sessions require honesty and willingness from all participants. They require an opening up of emotions. They should not be sessions of accusations or scenes of expressions of negative emotions. They should not become orgies of criticism, either of self or others.

Discuss calmly and with a sense of purpose those things or areas which seem to be causing family problems. Discover how realistic are these problems, and in what ways they can be handled. Supposed grievances often show up to be matters of lack of communication between family members. Hurt feelings are often caused by a lack of understanding of motivations.

Foolishly enough, a family that will have no hesitation about sitting down together to discuss a financial crisis or problem will not spend the same time to work out an emotional crisis or problem. Don't let embarrassment, pride, or self-isolation keep you and your family from achieving true family happiness. Use family therapy to handle problems of family living.

How the D. Family Used Family Therapy

"We use confrontation tactics regularly in our family," Mr. and Mr. D. explained. "We use it between ourselves, and we've taught our children to use it between themselves and with us."

Mrs. D. went on to say that she felt it had reduced tension and eliminated many possible areas of unhappiness in their family life.

"We are an active, creative family," Mr. D. said, "with differing temperaments and viewpoints. Two adults, three teen-agers, and two younger children add up to seven individuals!"

"Family therapy stops trouble before it starts," continued Mrs. D. "Grudges, brooding, jealousy, anxiety and misunderstanding can not flourish and grow in an atmosphere of open discussion."

The D. family had found that most causes of family disagreements and misunderstandings could be explained away by a positive, free expression of the problems.

"We have discovered," they said, "that most problems are

caused by a lack of understanding due to hasty conclusions. These hasty and wrong conclusions usually come from a lack of sufficient evidence or poor communication."

Mrs. D. gave a typical example. "Last week, Tim, our youngest boy, felt that his older brother Ron had deliberately taken advantage of the differences in their ages when he refused to take him ice-skating. Tim was upset and sulked about this. Later, when they discussed it, Ron explained that he had not taken him because he was going with a group of older boys and girls and thought Tim would feel left out, especially since he was a beginner on skates. He was planning to take him by himself and help him learn more about skating. In talking it over, both boys agreed that they had acted too hastily. Ron admitted that he should have explained his plans to Tim. Tim agreed that he was too quick to think he had been slighted by Ron, especially since his older brother had always been very considerate in the past."

The D. family concluded by saying that family therapy helped to keep them a happy, well-adjusted family. Minor irritations and problems did occur, but they did not get a chance to snowball into major angers or situations.

ADJUSTING TO CHANGES IN THE FAMILY GROUP

Because the family group is an organic structure, changes continually occur. The family is never static. Children grow up; parents grow older.

Breaks may appear in the family circle. These may be permanent as in divorce or death. They may be temporary as in illness, schooling, military service, or separations for economic reasons.

Any separation represents a change in family structure. Any change means a loss and anxiety. It requires adjustment from you.

The first step in adjusting to changes is to *acknowledge* them as possibilities and, when necessary, as actualities. Denying changes only adds to the tension.

The second step is to *accommodate* the changes. A mother whose children have left home must be willing to use the time she formerly spent on them for some new constructive purpose. A family who has lost a parent, either permanently or temporarily, must be willing to accept the situation by depending on the remaining parent or using a surrogate parent for the absent one.

Adjusting to changes in the family group requires individual responsibility. It also requires the recognition of group or family dependence. Adjustment means a mature response both as an individual and as a family. Adjustment means the acceptance of a fact of life. It is not a *denial* of the family, but an *affirmation.*

HOW TO WORK AND PLAY TOGETHER AS A FAMILY

A healthy family is one that is able to function adequately under *all* possible circumstances. One of the best ways to insure that healthy integration is to work and play together as a family.

A family becomes strengthened as a unit when the individual members learn to share an interest in a common project. Through sharing mutual responsibilities, each individual member matures as an individual as well as a member of the family.

Family recreation provides a needed climate for unobtrusive learning and maturing processes. Family relaxation is a time when possible tensions can be worked off in a healthy way.

Gardening is one possible family activity. Camping, hiking, bowling and other sports are also popular. Music or amateur dramatics can be the focal point of interest for a family.

It is not the particular type of activity that matters, it is the *bringing together* of the family and the *striving for a common goal* that are important.

A REMINDER

Since much of your personal happiness depends upon how well you get along with your family, you can't afford to neglect this area. "Being yourself" can be bad if it means being selfish and inconsiderate.

The successful family relationship demands self-discipline. Consideration should be a part of your family life.

Family therapy has proved to be an effective means of dealing with family problems and tensions.

Treat your family as you do your friends and enjoy harmony and happiness within your home.

12

The Crises of Accidents and Illness:
How to Handle Them and What
to Gain from Them

In this chapter I want to talk about how you can learn to face the hazards of living. More than that, I want to show you how you can cope with accidents or illness in your life. I want to show you how you can recognize and change an accident-prone personality.

Most people push aside the idea of disability even though they know it may happen to them. Like Shakespeare's Macbeth, they profess to believe "I lead a charmed life."

Unfortunately, few if any of us can *totally* escape the problems caused by accidents or illness. We can, however, prepare ourselves to accept these interruptions in our lives. Moreover, we can often gain from what might appear to be a hopeless or dead-end situation.

HOW ANGER CAN CAUSE ACCIDENTS

There are often two causes of accidents. One is the actual or readily apparent cause. The other cause is usually hidden and may be said to be the real cause.

John Smith is angry with his wife. They argue, and he leaves and goes out to work in the yard. He cuts his hand while pruning a tree. The *actual* or *apparent* cause of John Smith's accident is a slip of the pruning saw. The *real,* but *hidden* cause, is his anger with his wife.

How does anger cause accidents? It acts as a blinding force. How many times have you heard someone say, "I was so mad I couldn't see straight!" Have you said it yourself?

Being as angry as that means that you aren't going to see well enough to avoid an accident. This is when you run into a tree. This is when you hit your thumb and not the nail, or, like John Smith, saw your hand and not the tree limb.

Of course you are going to have accidents when you can't see what you are doing or where you are going. Anger acts like a blindfold!

HOW FEELINGS OF INFERIORITY CAN CAUSE ACCIDENTS

Feelings of inferiority can also cause accidents. An individual who feels that he is of little or no importance is not going to be particularly careful. Low self-esteem and carelessness go hand in hand—and usually they go to the emergency room!

"I never hire a workman who has a hangdog expression or dejected posture," a contractor told me. "That person may be a good workman, but I can predict from looking at him that he is going to have a series of minor accidents or perhaps one big accident. In any case, I can't afford to hire a source of potential trouble!"

Just as you tend to be careless with possessions of little or no value, so you can transfer that same attitude toward yourself.

How Peter Discovered the Cause of His Accidents

'I guess I'm just unlucky," Peter told me when I asked him why his fingers were bandaged. "I was lighting a cigarette when the whole package of matches caught on fire. I guess I forgot to close the cover of the matchbox."

Asked to catalog his recent past injuries, Peter came up with an impressive list of mishaps. He had had a sprained ankle because he failed to see a bottom step. An open cupboard door resulted in a black eye. An automobile accident accounted for two broken ribs and some facial lacerations.

"It doesn't really matter," Peter assured me. "I live alone so nobody's upset by what happens."

That was the clue to Peter's accidents. That was the reason for his self-appraised "bad luck." Peter had a strong feeling of inferiority because he was not successful in personality inter-relationships. Feeling that no one cared for him, he began to care less for himself. Each accident reinforced his self-image as an unworthy and unlikeable person.

Through treatment, Peter learned to raise the level of his self-esteem. He learned to appreciate himself as an individual and develop his own personality. He learned to evaluate his own good points and build a new self-image. He then learned to project that new self-image to others. He began to make friends.

As Peter's self-esteem rose, his accident level dropped.

SELF-PUNISHMENT MOTIVATIONS IN ACCIDENTS AND PSYCHOSOMATIC ILLNESSES

Despite our many scientific and technological advances, our basic moral codes have remained essentially the same. Thus we have a system whereby a bad deed (or sin) produces guilt and shame, and requires punishment.

The obvious flaws here are that not everyone has the same definition of sin or wrongdoing. Many people suffer torments of guilt for some supposed wrong deed or thought, while their neighbor might not be troubled by the same thing at all.

The guilty feeling needs some punishment in order to be *successfully* handled. We have a strong desire to exorcise this demon which we have permitted to lodge within ourselves. Since many of our guilty feelings are known only to ourselves, self-punishment is often a deep-seated but unconscious response. Accidents and psychosomatic illnesses are two of the most effective means of self-punishment.

Psychosomatic illness was discussed at length in Chapter 2 and the seven common psychosomatic symptoms were listed. These symptoms are headache, dizziness, breathing difficulties, psy-chosomatic heart problems, indigestion and stomach cramps, diarrhea, and sudden loss of sexual function.

Have you had any of these symptoms lately? Could it be because of a desire for self-punishment?

Two Typical Self-punishment Cases

Miriam didn't like her mother-in-law, but she felt she shouldn't have such feelings. Guilt caused her to develop severe headaches.

Analysis not only revealed the real cause of her headaches but it also helped her to bring her true feelings out into the open. Miriam learned that disliking her mother-in-law was not unnatural or "wicked." She then was able to go on and change her attitude toward her mother-in-law by having a more mature outlook. She learned to overlook and accept those aspects of her mother-in-law's character which had previously irritated her.

Miriam would never be terribly fond of her mother-in-law, but she had eliminated all feelings of guilt because she did not like her as well as she did other people. With the guilt gone, Miriam no longer had to punish herself with headaches.

You can not respond to each individual with the same degree of affection and warmth. Like Miriam, you must not let guilt trap you into self-punishing illnesses.

On his way home from a meeting, Ray ran into a tree and wrecked his new automobile. He could not give any explanation for the accident. He had not been sleepy. The road was clear. The automobile was mechanically perfect.

"It was just as if it was planned," Ray said. "It frightened me."

Ray was right—it *was* planned! It was planned by his unconscious desire for punishment.

"How were you punished as a child?" I asked him.

"My parents would take away a favorite toy," he said. "Usually it was a new one. Once I remember I disobeyed my father and he took away the sled I had just received as a birthday present."

"What are you doing now that you think your parents or your wife or friends wouldn't approve of? What are you doing that you feel is wrong?"

Ray hesitated and then admitted that he had been on the verge of having a love affair with his secretary.

"The night I wrecked my car, I had stopped at her apartment and had a drink. I was going to stay longer than I did but frankly, I felt so guilty that I left and started for home. I was very upset over what I had been thinking of doing."

Guilt drove Ray's car into the tree! He felt that he had done wrong by even considering an extramarital affair, and that he should be punished.

Following his childhood pattern of punishment, he wrecked his new "toy," his automobile. Ray had to learn that doing or thinking things that are contrary to self-imposed codes can result in serious consequences.

If you are uncomfortable with your actions, you are opening the door to trouble. You should analyze the reasons for your feelings of guilt. If they are unreasonable in basis or origin, learn to eliminate them as Miriam did. On the other hand, if they are understandable and are actually signals of impending disaster, alter your proposed conduct. This is particularly important in cases where your actions may harm not only yourself but others as well.

DISCOVERING SELF-PUNISHMENT MOTIVATIONS

Just as an insurance investigator will attempt to discover the causes of an accident, so you can investigate your own accident or illness. You can determine what part self-punishment motivations have played.

Ask yourself these questions:

1. *Preceding the onset of my accident or illness had I done anything that I would consider wrong?*

This could be something as obvious as an illegal or shady action or transaction. It could be a moral transgression. It could be a quarrel with someone, the telling of a lie, or a failure to do a required action. Whatever the cause, the immediate result was guilt.

2. *Immediately preceding my accident or illness was I contemplating some action, the actual performance of which I would regard as wrong?*

Some individuals suffer from guilt feelings because their thoughts are at wide variance with what they imagine people expect from them or the characters they believe themselves to be. They refuse to accept as *normal* those thoughts which are common to most people in times of stress, temptation, or anger. They assume unnecessary burdens of guilt.

3. *Was my accident or illness connected in some subtle way to my actual or supposed misdeed?*

In general, our *subconscious* tends to follow the "eye-for-an-eye" theory of punishment. Thus, we have such cases as the man who has been embezzling from his employer and accidentally cuts his fingers off while in his home workshop, or the unhappy housewife who has thought of running away from her family and accidentally spills a pot of hot soup on herself.

4. *Does the accident or illness punishment follow some recognizable childhood pattern of punishment?*

Does my accident or illness deprive me of something? Does it cause me physical pain? Does it make me an object of riducule or embarrass me in some way?

5. *Do I feel a sense of emotional or mental relief after my accident or upon becoming ill?*

Any amount of guilt can be relieved through the self-punishment device. The greater the guilt, however, the more punishment is demanded. Sometimes this punishment is changed to a series of accidents or illnesses.

HOW TO HANDLE THE ACCIDENT-PRONE CHILD OR ADULT

Children as well as adults, particularly emotionally immature adults, have a tendency to become accident prone because of guilt feelings and excessive feelings of hostility.

Resentment and fantasies of revenge frequently preoccupy the child's mind. After being reprimanded or punished by an adult, in particular by a parent, the child will have fantasies in which *he* punishes the *adult*. Often this will be a fantasy of physical torture or mistreatment resulting in the offending adult's pain, disfigurement, or disappearance. It is common for children to wish their parents would die. This is normal aggressive behavior.

This same pattern of angry, aggressive thoughts may occur among adults following a quarrel, particularly in marriage. Sometimes a grown son or daughter will have similar feelings when faced with an obstinate older parent.

Such feelings, although normal responses, often produce extreme feelings of guilt. It is particularly important to reassure children that such hostility and aggressive thoughts of revenge are *not* going to be punished. They should not be teased or ridiculed for these thoughts. They should be encouraged to discuss their feelings openly and made to understand that such thoughts are not dangerous, nor are they likely to actually *happen*. Small children have a belief in magic which is reinforced by fairy tales in which the wicked king and queen are deposed and put to death.

"I didn't get along with my older sister," Laura N. said. "I remember having fantasies in which she was killed or disappeared and I was the center of attention. One day she became ill. I can still remember how terrified I was. I was convinced that I was responsible. Fortunately my mother was a wise and understanding woman who, when I confessed my 'part' in my sister's illness, took time to explain that I couldn't be responsible. She didn't laugh at me or push me aside. We talked about jealousy and getting along as a family. Thanks to her attitude, I learned to understand my own emotions and not let guilt spoil my life."

As a mature individual, you do not need to be a slave to your guilt feelings. By understanding the *nature* of your guilt, you can keep it in proper perspective.

THE PARENT IMAGE AND ADULT BEHAVIOR IN ACCIDENT AND ILLNESS

Parents set the tone for adult behavior in accident and illness. It is their attitude toward accidents and illnesses which determines future adult response. The accident-prone child becomes the accident-prone adult. The child who learns to use illness as a weapon grows into the adult with psychosomatic illnesses.

The image of their parents is indelibly impressed upon most adults and still influences their responses, decisions, and reactions. When frequent accidents are accepted as normal behavior by parents, they continue to be acceptable throughout adult life.

If parents mistakenly insist that illness is a punishment for bad behavior, they make possible a continuing cycle of guilt and illness.

SICKNESS AND SEX

It is a mistaken belief that if you are sick, you can not enjoy an adequate sexual life. An individual who has had a good, mature sexual relationship before his illness is able to continue such a relationship. This is true even during a chronic, debilitating illness.

An individual who has feelings of guilt and considers that his illness is a punishment for evil, will give up his sexual life. He punishes himself by depriving himself of sex. He insists that he is too ill to enjoy a normal sexual life.

HOW TO DETERMINE IF YOU ARE ACTUALLY ACCIDENT PRONE

You can determine if you are accident prone by taking this test. Answer all the questions honestly. Only *you* can determine the level of your accident capability. Although we are talking specifically about accidents, the same questions apply to psychosomatic illness.

Write your answers down on a piece of paper so that after completing the test, you will have your *personal accident-prone report.*

Interpret the word "accident" to include any incident, however minor, in which there was either personal injury or a possibility of injury.

1. How many accidents have you had in the past year?
2. How many accidents have you had in the past 30 days?
3. Did you have an accident in the last 24-hour period? Did you have more than one?
4. Is your accident rate rising, constant, or falling?
5. How many of your accidents could be classified as major? (These are accidents that would require medical attention and perhaps involve some property damage.)
6. How many of your accidents could be classified as minor?
7. Has there been any change in your type of accident?
8. When do most of your accidents occur? Are there certain days or times of day which appear to be more hazardous for you?
9. Where do most of your accidents occur? Is it more dangerous for you to be at home than at work or vice versa? Are your accidents connected with your leisure-time activities?
10. What was the state of your emotions just preceding your accident? (It may help if you take one or two recent accidents and reconstruct the events leading up to the accident.)

11. Which of these words most closely describes your feelings just before the accident: *angry; guilty; worried; abstracted; nervous; arrogant?*
12. Were you trying to avoid something unpleasant?
13. What precise action did you take that caused the accident?
14. Was the accident actually caused by something you failed to do?
15. Could you have avoided the accident by choosing a different course of action?
16. Do you think the accident would have occurred if you had been in a different frame of mind?
17. After your accident did you feel relieved at having escaped some unpleasant or unwanted task or obligation?
18. After your accident, did you immediately place the blame on some other person or outside sources?
19. Where do you think you should have placed the blame?
20. Have you ever thought of suicide?

Your completed questionnaire should help you to understand and determine the level of your accident-prone capacity.

What Irving C. Learned Through the Accident-Prone Test

You may find the case of Irving C. helpful. In many ways, Irving was a typical accident-prone personality.

He came limping into my office on crutches. He had been injured in a fall. A machinist, he had tripped and fallen over a tool box.

"I just didn't see it," he explained. He went on to admit that he had had a series of accidents and that, in his words, he "felt jumpy."

Irving agreed to take the preceding accident-capability test. Here are the answers he gave to the questions.

1. Seven.
2. Three.
3. Yes. No.
4. Rising.
5. Four.

6. Three.
7. More major ones have occurred recently.
8. Weekdays. Mornings.
9. At work. More dangerous for me at work. No.
10. Upset.
11. Angry.
12. My foreman.
13. I took a short cut across the shop because I was in a hurry.
14. I guess I didn't watch where I was going.
15. Yes, if I had been on time for work, I wouldn't have gone a different way than my usual one.
16. No.
17. Yes. I was relieved that I could go to the dispensary instead of to my work station.
18. Actually, I blamed the poor guy who had put his tool box down there.
19. On myself, I suppose.
20. Occasionally.

Just taking the test and looking at his answers helped Irving to get a clearer picture of his accident-prone personality. It enabled him to get an understanding of the causes of his accidents.

In talking it over, Irving said, "I can see now that ever since the new foreman came, I have been upset."

A misunderstanding with the foreman when he first arrived had been the first difficulty. Then Irving felt that the foreman had gone out of his way to make things hard for him. On several occasions, he had criticized Irving's work in front of the other men.

"I hated to go to work," Irving said. "Some days I just felt sick."

"And some days you had accidents," I reminded him.

Fortunately an understanding company personnel office transferred Irving to another plant area. Once under a new foreman, Irving was able to do his work *without* accidents.

HOW TO CHANGE AN ACCIDENT-PRONE PERSONALITY

Can you change an accident-prone personality? *Yes.* You must look into your motivations—motivations that might have caused your accidents. Through self-analysis and guidance you can learn to understand your motivations.

Understanding is the first step. *Changing those motivations* is the second step. You may need to change your attitude, or your usual patterns of living.

Analyze your reactions to other people. Analyze your reactions to situations. Discover why some people and some situations have proved to be irritating and troublesome to you.

Do you have an adquate amount of self-esteem? The individual with adequate self-esteem has no need to resort to accidents. If you are accident prone, look for ways in which you can build up your self-esteem.

You can break the habit of unnecessary accidents!

UNDERSTANDING PSYCHOSOMATIC ILLNESSES

Psychosomatic illnesses, like unnecessary accidents. have their origin in emotional problems. They can be helped through treatment of the *causes* of the illnesses.

You should not be ashamed of a psychosomatic illness but you should not allow it to take over your life. Discovering the cause of your psychosomatic illness can help you eliminate it from your life.

Your emotional conflicts demand an outlet. One outlet may be a psychosomatic illness. Your psychosomatic symptoms are danger signals telling you that something is wrong. *You should be alerted to action by these symptoms.*

HOW TO ACCEPT THE PROBLEMS OF BONA FIDE ACCIDENTS AND ILLNESSES

Up to now we have been talking mostly about psychosomatic illnesses and unnecessary accidents, but there are *unavoidable* illnesses and accidents. I have called these *bona fide* illnesses and accidents.

Bona fide means *authentic* or *genuine.* These illnesses are not emotional in origin. These accidents are beyond control by the victim. However, these illnesses and accidents can cause emotional distress.

It is important that when you are ill or involved in an accident you do not feel guilty. Do not have self-punitive feelings about what has happened to you. It is also important that you do not allow yourself to become bitter or revengeful because of what has happened.

HOW TO ADJUST TO ACCIDENTS AND ILLNESSES IN THE FAMILY CIRCLE

Any interruption in family living patterns causes emotional distress. Any major breaks or changes in family routines are upsetting.

When one family member is the pivot member on which all things depend, there can be psychological problems when that person becomes ill or disabled. All the dependent family members feel threatened. They feel that their happiness and welfare comes from that person. They have a sense of loss of happiness and well-being.

It is not unusual for sickness in the family, especially the sickness of a key member, to produce an atmosphere of anger, disappointment, and depression.

"My husband gets so irritated when I get sick," a neighbor told me.

It was obvious that her husband saw his wife as a mother-figure and himself as dependent upon her for his welfare, particularly for the basic comforts. He experienced the same feelings of anger and unhappiness that a small child feels when his mother is unable to take care of him.

Life in the family must go on despite accidents or illness. There should be an emphasis on mutual concern and dependence on the part of well members. Family responsibilities should be reapportioned and shared.

Explanations of adult accidents or illnesses should be given to children. This, however, should be in terms that they can understand. This is particularly important if a parent is no longer able to function in the usual way or must be hospitalized. Many adults report traumatic childhood experiences when one of their parents became ill and they did not understand what had happened.

"My father suddenly changed one day and didn't play ball or

joke with us anymore," one man told me. "I was told not to bother him. I thought he was angry with me and didn't want me. I was several years older before I found out that he had developed a heart condition. It would have been much better if my father had explained it to me when I was little. I might not have understood the medical angle, but I would not have felt unloved and rejected!"

REGRESSION IN ILLNESS

It will be helpful to you in adjusting to illness, either your own or that of others, to understand the part regression plays at such times. Regression, which is a return to a childlike state, is a natural happening in any illness or convalescence period.

Regression has a *positive* part to play in illness. An ill person feels helpless, passive and like a child. This is good, for that passivity and childlike willingness to accept care is necessary for rest and the healing process.

Since this childlike dependence is a part of getting well, it should be accepted by the patient and understood by those who must care for him. Accepting this regressive attitude as one part of the healing treatment will be an aid to recovery.

HOW TO COPE WITH YOUR OWN ACCIDENT OR ILLNESS

When "It can't happen to me" becomes changed to "It did happen to me," you have to adjust your own emotional attitudes.

Illness means a change in your routine. It means a change in your activities. It may mean a change in your relationships with others. No matter what the changes, you are going to have to learn to accept them. Not accepting them will only add to your problems. It will lengthen and complicate your period of recovery.

There are six steps you can take to help you cope with your own accident or illness.

SIX STEPS TO HELP YOU IN YOUR ILLNESS
OR ACCIDENT SITUATION

1. *Accept the fact of your accident or illness as present reality.*

Don't waste time wishing it hadn't happened It *has,* so go on from there.

2. *Understand the nature of your illness or disability, including its limitations and possibilities.*

Ignorance and fear can cause you more pain and unhappiness than any physical symptom. Limitations and possibilities are only guidelines to help you develop a new way of living.

3. *Adopt positive attitudes.*

You will be a happier individual if you adopt *positive* attitudes. Other people will like you better also. We all try to avoid the complainer or whiner. *Negative* attitudes of guilt, complaints, anger, irritation, or despair poison your life. Your personality reflects that poisoning project. Just as a plant would die under similar circumstances, your personality will wilt. It will be unpleasant, unlovable.

4. *Be willing to change your life.*

Disability or illness may mean some drastic changes in the way you live—changes in your habits—changes in the way you do things. Despite your limitations, you can often have as full and complete a life as you had before your illness. You must be willing, however, to make changes and to accept different ways of doing things. These changes may include such routine matters as dressing, eating, or household tasks. You may have to choose different recreational activities.

"After my accident, I thought my life as a housewife and mother was over," Mrs. J. said. "I knew I would have to be in a wheel-chair and I thought that I would just be a helpless invalid. Thanks to a sensible doctor and a patient and understanding family, I learned that it wasn't the end of my life. I've learned to cook, keep house, and care for my two youngsters all from my wheelchair. Yes, it is a different life, but it is an active life and a normal family life."

5. *Apply the law of compensation.*

If you have had to give up one skill because of your accident or illness, you can develop another skill. If you have stopped one activity, you can start another. If you can not pursue one interest, you can develop a new one. The world is full of stories of men and women who discovered unexpected resources and talents when circumstances forced changes upon them.

6. *Look for opportunities for service to others.*

An illness or an accident need not limit your capacity to be of service to others. Feeling more useful as a person will help you. It will raise your self-esteem and keep it at a high level.

HOW MUCH CAN BE LEARNED AND HOW NEW MATURATIONAL LEVELS CAN BE REACHED AS A RESULT OF CRISES

Crises can be a means of learning the importance of living a full and useful life. Major illnesses or disabilities frequently result in a more creative attitude toward life. They frequently precipitate changes in motivation.

Many famous men and women have enjoyed their successful careers after some illness or accident forced a change of plans upon them or gave them a deep sense of purpose. One outstanding example is that of Franklin D. Roosevelt, who despite his physical handicaps from polio became President of the United States and a world-renowned leader during World War II.

Crisis can bring a family closer together. It can bring forth concern and love; it can be a uniting force. Crisis can be turned into a *positive* event.

Crisis in your personal life can be a strengthening force. You should regard a major crisis as an invitation to a second chance at making your life more meaningful.

Consider crisis as opportunity!

A REMINDER

When you feel yourself close to danger points of anger, irritation, or emotional blindness, stop and think about your actions. Proceed slowly. Analyze your motivations.

Accept personal responsibility for your actions, but avoid feelings of guilt. Don't punish yourself.

Free yourself from the tyranny of frequent accidents. Don't handicap yourself by having psychosomatic illnesses.

Adjust to unavoidable accidents or illnesses. Resist self-pity. Keep your self-esteem high.

Learn to live a normal life within the bounds of your disability. Learn to have a happy, useful life.

Don't be overwhelmed by crisis. *Let crisis work for you, not against you.*

13

How to Overcome Loneliness

Loneliness is a common problem which can affect any one of us. It can affect *you.* It can affect you at different periods in your life, and it can affect you in different ways.

As a psychiatrist, I see the bad effects that loneliness can have on the individual personality. It is a disabling disease. which can strike any person. No matter what your age, profession, or economic status, *loneliness can touch you.*

There are no immunization shots that can be taken to keep it away. However, in this chapter I am going to show you how you can *cure* yourself of the *crippling* effects of loneliness.

LIVING ALONE IN MODERN SOCIETY

Living alone in modern society is not easy. This is a group social culture in which we live. Getting along with others is stressed. Teamwork is stressed.

You move through life in groups. You work with others. You are in classes in school. At least a part of your leisure hours may be spent in some kind of group activity, such as bowling. You also take part in group activity when you are a spectator at a sporting event—or attend a concert, a theatrical performance, religious services—or stand on the curb to cheer a parade.

But what are you going to do when these activities end and you must go home alone? If you live by yourself, you must not succumb to loneliness.

I am not going to pretend to you that loneliness does not exist. It *does*. I am not saying that it *is* not a problem. I do say that it does not *need* to be a problem.

You can learn to overcome loneliness.

BE FRIENDS WITH YOURSELF

Be friends with yourself. You can't be happy if you are alone with someone you don't like or respect.

Enjoy yourself as a person. Keep yourself mentally alert through reading. Adopt a hobby that will give you hours of pleasure.

Remember that if *you* find *yourself* interesting, others will find you interesting also.

Treat yourself right! Make your surroundings pleasant and convenient for yourself. Don't skimp or refuse to take time for yourself. Remember—you can be the honored guest in your own home.

How Sharon Stopped Short-changing Herself

Sharon worked in a large office but lived alone in a small but adequate apartment. She consulted me because she was getting increasingly depressed.

I noticed that although an attractive girl, she had not taken much time with her appearance. Frown lines creased her forehead, and a stranger would have taken her to be much older than she actually was.

"My apartment is so depressing," she complained. "I used to like it when I first moved there but now it seems gloomy and sad."

She admitted that she didn't keep it up as she had when she first moved there.

"I'm too tired these days," she said, "and besides, what's the point, I mean, just for me!"

"That is the whole point," I told her. "*Just* for you!"

Sharon wasn't interested when I talked to her about what she was doing to herself. She refused to admit that she was short-changing herself.

"All I need are some tranquilizers," she insisted. "Please give me a prescription, Doctor."

"First, I'd like to give you a prescription for something else, but you must promise to follow my directions exactly."

Sharon promised, and I handed her a prescription slip on which I had written these words. "One dozen yellow daffodils. Place them in a container in a conspicuous spot in your apartment."

Before she could object, I reminded her of her promise. I asked her to return to my office in a week.

A week later when Sharon kept her appointment, she was a new person. The frown lines were gone. She looked younger. Her attitude was joyful. She was tastefully dressed.

"You are a miracle worker!" she exclaimed.

"No," I answered, "you have worked your own miracle. I only started you out."

Sharon then described to me what had happened. She had bought the daffodils and taken them home.

"I put them in a vase on an end table," she said, "and then I sat down to rest as usual. The flowers were so pretty that I kept looking at them. I noticed then how cluttered the apartment was so I got up and straightened things up."

Instead of her usual pickup supper, she prepared a regular meal for herself.

"I had moved the flowers to my dining table and it seemed a shame not to set the table properly," Sharon explained. "I even got out some candles. After such a pleasant meal," she continued, "it seemed a shame not to do something interesting. I had always been curious about weaving and had, in fact, bought a small hand loom weaving kit. However, I had stored it in the closet because I couldn't seem to get enough energy to work on it."

Sharon described how she had gotten out the kit and started using it. Now she had several weaving projects in mind.

"I can hardly wait to get home after work," she said. "My apartment has become so pleasant that I miss it when I'm away."

If you live alone—what would a bouquet of flowers do for you?

RESPONSES TO LONELINESS

Loneliness as a psychological condition affects the personality. It demands some kind of response from the individual.

There are positive and negative responses to loneliness. *You* are the one who decides which response, positive or negative, you are going to make. The choice you make will determine your happiness and usefulness in life.

Negative responses are retreats from reality. They may appear to you as the only solution to your problem of loneliness. Often they will, on the surface, appear to be the easiest way. This is a false impression that you are receiving.

You must avoid settling for less than that which will make you happy. Only positive responses to loneliness can do this.

SIX NEGATIVE RESPONSES TO LONELINESS

There are six common negative responses to loneliness:

1. Alcoholism
2. Drugs
3. Food
4. Hypochondria
5. Childish or anti-social behavior
6. The death wish

Have you taken or been tempted to take one of these negative courses of action in response to your loneliness?

These are *not* solutions to your problem!

HOW TO AVOID NEGATIVE RESPONSES TO LONELINESS

By learning what these negative responses to loneliness are, you have taken the first step toward positive responses. Recognition of these negatives is one way of avoiding them. Knowing that they are undesirable, you can change the direction of your thought and actions to positive ways.

Imagine that you are playing a game of life decisions and responses to life problems. You are standing before a board on which are printed multiple choices, some negative. some positive. *Which ones will you pick?*

Now imagine that whenever you pick a negative response, you receive an unpleasant shock to your system. A positive response on the other hand, means you will receive a tangible reward-something you want: money, friends success, love—rewards of enjoyment from positive choices.

In *your* game of life, what do *you* want? Will *your* choices give you rewards or the jolt of unpleasant shocks?

Avoid the negative responses. Claim the rewards of a happy life.

How Carl Overcame His Dependence on Alcohol

It was obvious that Carl needed help when he walked into my office. He was thin, worried, shaking, and extremely nervous. At first, he would not admit why he had come to see me other than to say that he "needed help."

Yes, he did need help, and it took time to make him into the healthy, happy, and successful citizen he is today.

Carl's story is not unusual. A busy, minor executive in a large company and living alone, he was basically very lonely. In an effort to forget his loneliness, Carl turned to alcohol.

"When I started," he said, "it was just one or two drinks. It really seemed to relax me. I felt less lonely."

Alcohol gave Carl a false sense of security. Unfortunately the effect didn't last and he soon found himself drinking more. His periods of sobriety became shorter and less bearable.

"I am doubly miserable now," Carl said when he consulted me. "I feel lonelier than before, yet I keep drinking because I don't know what else to do."

Carl was caught in a vicious circle. He drank because he was lonely, yet he also realized that his dependency on alcohol isolated him from others. He looked at himself with loathing and regarded his future with horror. He needed to break out of that circle.

With the help of analysis, and because he was willing to try, Carl did find a way out. Stopping the drinking would aid Carl's physical health, which was deteriorating because of his overuse of alcohol, but it would not cure the *emotional* problem, loneliness, that was responsible.

Carl began a program of working to help others. He had formerly been a college basketball star. Soon he was putting that knowledge to use by coaching a team of boys at a community center. From coaching, Carl got the feeling of acceptance that he needed—a feeling he had never gotten from his work.

Carl developed an interest in other facets of the community center program. He became a leader of an adult education group.

Yes, Carl broke out of his circle and changed his life. If you are caught in such a circle, you, too, can find *your* way out.

The secret to getting out is to involve yourself in helping others. *Try it!*

DRUGS ARE NOT THE ANSWER

The use of drugs is no longer confined to any one segment of our population. Young people, in particular, have turned eagerly to drugs. It is estimated that at least 20 percent of U. S. college students have experimented with drugs in some form.

The age limits of drug users have now spread into a wide spectrum that has pre-teen-agers at one end and middle-aged persons at the other end. We are rapidly becoming a drug-oriented civilization, but drugs are *not* the answer to the problems of living.

Loneliness, which is one common excuse for using drugs, is not cured but is compounded by drugs. The drug addict becomes more isolated, more alienated from the real world, the world in which he has to live.

Using drugs only postpones an inevitable reckoning. If you use drugs or are tempted to use them—*don't! They are not the answer to your loneliness.*

You can get "high" on helping others. Instead of smoking a joint or taking a trip, try using your time and talents for others.

How Mrs. K. Got Off the Treadmill of Overeating

Mrs. K. came to me because she was depressed and lonely. A woman in her fifties who had lived alone for a number of years since her husband's death, Mrs. K. had another problem which she didn't mention—but which she couldn't hide. This was *obesity,* or, to put it in plain language, Mrs. K. was *too fat.*

Eating to compensate for loneliness is common. Children do it, adolescents do it, adults do it, and so do the aged.

"When I feel sad or don't know what to do, I have a little snack or fix a meal," confessed Mrs. K. "It always cheers me up."

Yes, eating does have that effect. You are doing something for yourself, something you like. This becomes even more important when you feel alone or neglected. You are trying to induce a sense of well-being and love into your life by eating. You have disguised your hunger pains for companionship as hunger pains for food. Unfortunately, food won't satisfy your needs; it only increases them.

This is what had happened to Mrs. K. Food was the prime interest in her life. I noticed, however, that she was interested not only in eating food but also in preparing it. I suggested that she use this interest.

"Why don't you share your interest in food with other people?" I asked her.

Mrs. K. replied that she didn't know how she could, and furthermore she felt too shy to approach strangers. She did finally agree to try my suggestions.

I put her in touch with two local organizations that could use and benefit from her interest in food. One was a service club that had recently started a program of providing hot meals for the aged and shut-ins. The other was an organization which placed foreign visitors in American homes for short-term visits and a sampling of American food and customs.

Mrs. K's initial shyness and nervousness wore off as she became involved in her new activities. She began to lose weight because she was *too busy* to take time out for her extra little snacks. She had gotten off her treadmill of overeating and *was going somewhere* with her life.

HYPOCHONDRIA AS A SUBSTITUTE FOR FRIENDS

Hypochondria is another negative response to loneliness. Hypochondria, which is *a morbid preoccupation with your health*, does not make you less lonely. As with any of the negative responses, it will only fill up a *part* of your time and attention. Your problem of loneliness is still there. *It is not solved.*

You not only feel miserable when you are so concerned about your health but you also present an unattractive personality to others. You repulse people who do not share your interest in your state of health.

Hypochondria can not really take the place of friends in your life. It is an unsatisfactory substitute for friendship.

HOW TO COPE WITH LONELINESS CAUSED BY DEATH OF A SPOUSE OR OTHER LOVED ONE

Death does more than rob us of someone we love; it often robs us of our own life force. Perhaps one of the biggest causes of loneliness is the death of a spouse or other loved one. Yet life does not stop for the survivor.

"I wish I were dead too!" sobbed a recent widow.

Her friends were shocked, but she was only giving vent to a common expression of grief. The death wish is there in most people, but remains buried until things go wrong. Like children running away from home in the face of trouble, adults will try or at least express a desire to run away from life. There is only *one* way to run away from life, and that is to die.

Most people rally eventually after the emotional shock of loss by death has subsided. They have learned that *life must be lived.* If you are lonely because of such a loss, you can learn to overcome that loneliness.

There are people who need you. There are things you can still do with your life. To give in to grief is no credit to the person you loved and with whom you shared a life. To wallow in loneliness and withdraw from life is no solution.

I once shocked a woman out of her prolonged and useless period of grief by asking her, "What would your husband say to you if he could see you crying here in my office? What would he say if he heard you complain of your loneliness?"

She stopped crying and thought for a few minutes. "He'd tell me to stop whining and get busy," she admitted.

"And can you?" I asked her.

"I'll try."

She did try—and although I know that there were times of bleak despair when it wasn't easy for her, she succeeded in overcoming her grief and loneliness.

Death is real, and it brings real loneliness. That loneliness can be cured by keeping busy. Grief and loneliness wither in an atmosphere of activity.

HOW TO ADJUST TO LONELINESS CAUSED BY PERSONAL ILLNESS

Illness often causes personality changes. Many times these changes occur because of *loneliness.* Basically, this is a world of good health, and the individual who is sidelined by illness feels left out of life. The period of enforced idleness and isolation because of illness can be an emotionally traumatic experience. When that illness becomes a permanent disability, the gravity of the emotional problem radically increases.

No one wants to be ill if he is emotionally mature. You don't want to be ill. I don't want to be ill. However, illness can and often does come into our lives.

Although you may be cut off from your work and other usual activities because of illness, you can adjust to your altered circumstances. Do not be preoccupied solely with yourself. The concern of your family and friends, the care you are receiving, may lead you into thinking that the world is centered in yourself. *No, the world is not.* The world is going on. Your family and friends are living their lives. They have to. You too must live a life despite your illness. True, your life, your activities, your plans will be dictated and circumscribed by the extent of your illness or disability, but you can not afford the luxury of misery and self-pity. Even from a hospital bed you can be of service to others. If you can use your hands, there are practically no limits to what you can do. A woman I know makes baby clothes for families less fortunate. *"Less fortunate,"* she says although she herself is in the hospital with severe leg injuries from an accident.

Another man, although confined to bed for several months with a chronic disabling illness, still found time each day to write several letters to servicemen stationed in Viet Nam and to wounded veterans. "My pain never seems as severe when I am writing. I know how difficult and lonely it must be for them."

If you are a shut-in because of a physical disability, start a small home business. Decide what your talent is, and then *use it.* A man I know who is not able to go outside and work does leatherwork. A woman who can sit up only a few hours a day manages to use those few hours to paint pictures. The real profit in those ventures is not in dollars and cents but in the feeling of being a part of the world again.

If you are ill or disabled, enlarge your *mental* and *emotional* boundaries and the physical boundaries which you must accept will no longer seem so confining.

HOW TO OVERCOME LONELINESS CAUSED BY MOVING
TO A NEW PLACE

Some people like to move. They are explorers at heart. Most of us, however, experience some degree of loneliness when we move to a new place. This loneliness is a result of leaving friends, perhaps family, behind. It is caused by the strange and unfamiliar surroundings in which we find ourselves.

You can overcome that loneliness in two ways. One involves a preparation period before the actual move. The other concerns your attitude and activities *after* the move.

When your family is involved in a move, it is important that *each member* understand the reason for the move and be prepared for it. Children especially sometimes have difficulty in understanding why they must leave their home, school, and playmates. A clear explanation of the "why" of moving will do much to help them over this period of anxiety.

The preparation period for moving should also include discussions about the new location, the new housing, and the advantages to be found in the new area. This psychological preparation will do much to shorten the period of loneliness after the move.

Once you are located in your new place, try to become a member of the new community as soon as possible. Join the church of your choice. Transfer club or lodge memberships. If your town has a Newcomer's Club, attend the meetings. When you are settled, become involved in some kind of community work.

Your period of loneliness will be shortened in proportion to your willingness to become a *concerned* individual in your new community.

How The B. Family Adjusts to Frequent Moves

Jim B. is a construction engineer whose firm frequently moves him to new locations. Despite this, the B. family is a happy and contented one with no psychological or emotional problems. I asked Mrs. B. how she and her husband handle this, particularly in reference to their four children.

"Moving in all its phases is a family affair with us," she said. "No, we are not always eager to leave our home, friends, school and church, but we know that because of Jim's work, moving often is our way of life. We do try to make it as pleasant a possible."

Asked for specific examples, Mrs. B. went on to say, "Fortunately we usually know about the impending move for several weeks in advance. As soon as my husband is notified, we have a family conference. We explain to the children *why* we are moving, *when,* and *where.* In the weeks to come, we not only pack but we also try to learn all we can about our new location. I get books and magazine articles from the public library which will help us all to learn the history and facts about our new location. We subscribe to the local paper of the new town and by reading it we become familiar with civic issues, current city happenings, names of stores, schools and churches. I send to the Chamber of Commerce and get information and a city map. We study the map and the names of the streets. Once we have decided on a place to live, we concentrate on learning the names of the streets in our immediate area and the location of shops, schools, the library, and church. If possible, we take the children with us for a pre-move visit while we look for housing.

"The result of all this preparation," she continued, "is that none of us feel too strange when we finally move. If the surroundings are not too familiar, at least the names, the location, and the history are. It doesn't take us long to settle down."

"Do you do anything special once you have moved?" I asked her.

"Yes," she explained, "for I know that in spite of all our preparation, there will be moments of loneliness and anxiety for all of us. After all, we will be missing our friends, we will have to learn new patterns of living. We do try to help this by joining a church right away and enrolling the children in Sunday School. This is a big help to them in making new friends. Jim is active in his lodge and he continues that in our new city. I transfer my membership in the two national clubs to which I belong. Jim and I make it a point to spend extra time with the children during this period of adjustment. We also plan special family trips to explore the resources of our new area. For example, when we moved to this town we visited, as a family, the art museum, the zoo, the historical museum, the public library and we went camping at the nearby lake. *We move as a family.*"

Yes, the B. family had found a successful way to overcome the loneliness of moving to a new place. You can do the same for yourself and your family.

HOW TO COPE WITH THE LONELINESS CAUSED BY A NEW JOB

There's a *special* kind of loneliness that is caused by a new job. In some ways, it is similar to that caused by moving to a new town. Often the two occur simultaneously, as a move to a new area may mean a new job. You can cope with this loneliness by analyzing the reasons for it and then taking care of each reason by some *positive* action.

Loneliness is sometimes caused simply because you are the stranger and everybody else knows the names and stories of the others. You feel left out because your are the newcomer. This can be solved by various positive actions. First you, yourself, must be friendly and outgoing to the others in your new place of business. Make it easy for people to be friends with you. Make a special effort to remember names and facts about those with whom you work. Show an interest in them and their lives. A good device for getting acquainted is to ask for information about local customs, shops, and recreational areas. If your company has an employee recreational program, sign up for it. If your company has a civic responsibility as charitable work, take part. *Don't wait to be asked, step up and volunteer.*

You may feel lonely because you are suffering from anxiety over whether or not you can do your new job properly. There are ways to cope with this. Assure yourself that you would not have been offered this new position if your employer had had doubts about your capability. Some of your problem may come from an uncertainty about your new duties. Be sure that you understand what your job is. *Don't be afraid to ask.* Learn all you can about what you are to do. Feeling familiar and capable in your job will eliminate your fear and sense of isolation.

HOW TO HANDLE LONELINESS IN CHILDREN

Olive Schreiner in her book, *The Story of an African Farm,* wrote, "The barb in the arrow of childhood suffering is this: its intense loneliness, its intense ignorance."

I am sure that all of us can remember periods of extreme loneliness which we suffered as children. In some cases, those experiences may have affected our adult behavior.

Children are at the mercy of adults. They are dependent upon the adult world. Children are not creatures who do not worry or wonder. They are concerned about life, about their family, and particularly about themselves. They do become anxious about family problems, economic security, and their own future.

Loneliness in children is usually caused by parental neglect or indifference. It may be caused by physical differences which keep the child away from normal childhood activities. It is often caused by a lack of understanding of adult motivations and plans.

You can handle loneliness in children by treating them as individuals. *Listen to your child when he talks to you.* Listen carefully to his fantasy tales. He may be trying to tell you something about his loneliness.

Help your child to make friends. Encourage him to have and develop a hobby. Make it possible for him to join an organized youth group.

Show your interest in your children by visiting their schools, going to special programs in which they have a part, and serving when necessary as an adult sponsor of their club activities.

Make your child or children feel *wanted*. Don't be afraid to discuss common household problems in their presence. They may surprise you by their quick grasp of the situation.

Why Steve Was Lonely

A mother and father consulted me about their young son, Steve. Steve, only eight years old, was already in serious trouble at school because of malicious behavior.

After talking to Steve and his parents, the reason for Steve's behavior was clear. The boy was *lonely.* He had destroyed property and had become insolent to his teachers and other adults and anti-social in his relations with his playmates. He was expressing his loneliness in the only way he knew—*bad behavior.*

Steve's parents were busy prople. They both worked and were active in civic, club, and social organizations. They were gone from home much of the time, leaving Steve in the care of a maid.

"But Steve has everything," his mother protested when I said Steve was suffering from loneliness and neglect.

Yes, Steve *seemed* to have everything. His parents gave him a good home, well-balanced meals, all sorts of toys and a good school. What they did not give him was real love, concern and

interest. Until they consulted me, they did not realize that Steve
had everything *but parents.*

Fortunately for Steve, they were willing to change their pattern
of living to include Steve. They began to live and play together as
a family.

HOW TO AVOID LONELINESS WHEN YOU ARE OLDER

Growing older sometimes brings special problems of loneliness.
Children grow up and move away. They become involved in their
own family affairs. Husbands and wives die. Professional and work
responsibilities may cease with retirement.

You can avoid the loneliness caused by these changes in your
life if you will prepare in advance for them. Have some other
interest besides your family or job. Develop an absorbing hobby, a
social or charitable interest. Widen the scope of your interests so
that you are not dependent upon one thing to keep you from
being lonely.

There are many places that welcome the help of the older
experienced citizen. There are clinics that need volunteers to help
with the paper work, to help the medical personnel, or to work
with patients. There are child care centers, institutions for the
retarded, hospitals for the mentally ill, and homes for the aged
where assistance is needed.

Because as an older person you have more free time and less
pressing family responsibilities, you can serve your community—
and indirectly, *help yourself.*

HOW YOU CAN CHANGE YOUR CHILDISH REACTIONS TO MATURE
ONES AND AVOID LONELINESS

Loneliness often triggers childish and immature reactions. Some
of these childish reactions are complaining, whining, refusing to
take part in things, not wanting to believe in the facts of your life
and blaming others for your loneliness.

If you have reacted in any of these ways, then you are not
helping your loneliness. By not behaving as an adult, you are
cutting yourself off from other adults and *increasing* your
loneliness.

Change your complaints to compliments. If a neighbor comes to visit, don't spend time complaining about your life; instead look for some way in which you can compliment your visitor. Extend this idea to your own personality. For example, change your inner dialogue from "I don't see why I have to be alone," to "My, you do make good cookies."

Change whining to work. If, as in the example above, you are a good baker, don't waste time whining about your loneliness—bake a batch of cookies. Get dressed and take some cookies to your neighbor or to a shut-in.

Don't waste time in self-pity. Don't poison your life by refusing to make the best of what you have and what you are. A morbid preoccupation with yourself only isolates you from the others you need.

You are an adult; you wouldn't throw yourself on the floor and have a tantrum, would you? You'd be too ashamed to behave in such a childish fashion. So why have mental and emotional tantrums?

Stand on your feet and face the world in an *adult* way. You will be pleased and surprised at the way the world looks back at you.

HOW YOU CAN CURE YOUR FEELINGS OF LONELINESS BY THOUGHTS AND ACTS OF CONCERN AND LOVE TOWARD OTHERS

One of the best descriptions of *loneliness* was written by a Ninth Century Japanese poet, Ono No Komachi.

> So lonely am I
> My body is a floating weed
> Severed at the roots.

This is the way many people feel when they are lonely. A deep sense of loss and of isolation hits them. They feel set apart from other people.

If you feel this way, if you feel that nobody understands you, that nobody loves you, and you have no friends, then you are suffering from loneliness. You can cure those feelings and change all of these statements to *positive* assertions of understanding, love, and friendship.

The cure for loneliness is involving yourself with other people.

The change in your life comes about through your thoughts and acts of concern and love toward others. Put aside your shyness, your fears of rejection and inadequacy, and go out and *extend your hands in help.* You can do this through aiding one person or a group of people. You can work with hospitals, nursing homes, welfare societies, service clubs, and other groups. There are groups in every town who need your assistance.

You have a talent to be *used.* You have a life to be *shared.* You will go out to strangers—and find friends.

Don't ask for help—give help!

A REMINDER

You can overcome loneliness by taking positive actions and making positive responses.

Don't isolate yourself from others by being overly concerned about yourself.

Be friends with yourself, and others will find it easy to be friends with you also.

Help yourself by helping others.

Few people *choose* to live alone, but often they have no choice. If you have to live alone and don't especially like it, *you can still be happy!*

14

How to Live with a Person Having Emotional Problems

Neurotic symptoms and behavior are not unusual. They do exist in a large number of people. As modern living becomes more complicated, more noisy, and more filled with stress situations, neurotic symptoms increase.

You may have a member of your family, a close friend or business associate who is neurotic. You may have difficulty in getting along with this person. Even when you realize that he can not help his actions and attitudes, you may find that you respond in irritation.

Living or working with a person who has a neurotic personality is not easy. It produces strain and tension. Often there are misunderstandings which are difficult to clear up satisfactorily.

In this chapter, I am going to show you how you can help both yourself and the other person. You do not need to continue to suffer from frustration and unhappiness because of your relationship with a person who has emotional problems.

WHAT DO WE MEAN BY A NEUROTIC?

A neurotic is a person who has emotional problems. He is a person who is living in a *conflict* situation which is affecting his *personality*. He is emotionally disturbed but not mentally deranged. He is handicapped by his neurotic personality, but not totally disabled. He functions *in spite of* his emotional problems. He does not function to his best capabilities, however. Just as an automobile will not perform well on a few cylinders, so a person with emotional problems can not perform his life duties adequately.

A neurotic is not a happy person. His emotional problems keep him from his happiness. A neurotic does not get along well with his family or other people. He projects his emotional problems and his unhappiness into his interpersonal relationships.

A neurotic needs understanding and help.

HOW TO RECOGNIZE THE SYMPTOMS OF NEUROTIC BEHAVIOR

It is important to be able to recognize the symptoms of neurotic behavior. In general, a neurotic shows or has *erratic, eccentric,* or *obsessive* behavior patterns. These symptoms may be present in varying degrees. At first, they may not be readily perceptible. Often the person himself does not recognize the beginnings of neurotic symptoms.

Look for any personality changes. Look for symptoms of anxiety, tenseness, chronic fatigue, irritability or outbursts of anger. Other symptoms are sudden concern with personal health, insomnia, or expressions of hostility. This hostility can be directed toward individuals or toward institutions, certain classes of people or ideas.

Irrational fears are a symptom of neurotic behavior. So is any form of obsessive or compulsive reaction. The person with emotional problems may develop an obsession with neatness or perfection. He may feel compelled to repeat certain actions, gestures, or words.

In most cases, the neurotic person is not hiding his symptoms. You may be deliberately *overlooking* symptoms because you do not want to admit them into your consciousness.

CHECK LIST OF NEUROTIC SYMPTOMS

If you suspect that someone with whom you are closely associated may be suffering from emotional problems, look over this check list of neurotic symptoms.

My family member, friend or associate has:

1. Become tense.
2. Complained of being continually tired.
3. Become irritable without apparent cause.
4. Complained of physical ills or pains.
5. Been unable to sleep.
6. Exhibited new, excessive dislikes.
7. Appeared to be guilty or fearful.
8. Developed some unusual obsessions or compulsions.
9. Shown signs of anxiety.

Any *one* or any *combination* of these symptoms can be present.

CAUSES OF NEUROTIC BEHAVIOR

Just as a cold, an infection, or a sprain is caused by some agency or event, so emotional disturbances have a cause. They do not just happen without cause. They may appear to be unrelated to any event or happening, but this is false. They *do* have origins.

Some of the causes are very obvious. Such events as the death of a loved one, the loss of a job, physical illness, or an accident can result in neurotic behavior. Emotional disturbances can also be caused by real or imagined lack of success in business or professional life. They can be caused by romantic problems or by social situations.

Traumatic experiences are the usually accepted causes for neurotic behavior. This is natural since they are not only the most obvious but also the most understandable. An individual is *expected* to react in some way to such an experience. When that reaction persists, however, the person is behaving neurotically. When that reaction is too intense for the cause, it is a sign of emotional trouble.

Many people overlook the fact that so-called "good" things can also be causes of neurotic behavior. Any sudden change in an individual's status or situation is capable of producing emotional disturbances. This is true even when it is a change that should result in joy and increased happiness. For example, a job promotion, a new position, parenthood or some club office can produce neurotic behavior.

One patient, I remember, became very neurotic following the

birth of his first grandchild. He became a compulsive talker, and developed insomnia and chest pains.

Analysis revealed that he equated the birth of his grandchild with his own aging. It was also brought out that my patient feared death. His own father had died shortly after my patient's first child had been born. The two events had become fused in his mind. With the birth of his own grandchild, he began to both fear and anticipate his own death.

WHY NEUROTIC SYMPTOMS OCCUR

A common question that is frequently asked is why do some people develop neurotic symptoms while others do not?

The same conditions of stress do not have the same effect upon individuals. Some individuals are better able to handle stress, shock, or sudden change. However, these traumatic conditions will expose any *weak* or *faulty* behavior patterns or thoughts. Latent fears, conflicts, or feelings of guilt will come to the surface.

Just as some machines can stand hard usage and strain while others break down, so people vary in their ability to successfully withstand stress.

Neurotic symptoms are like tire blowouts. And, as in blowouts, the damage done will depend upon the circumstances and upon the skill of the individual. If he can keep from losing control, there will be a minimum of damage.

HOW TO DISCOVER THE SITUATIONAL PROBLEMS THAT CAUSE EMOTIONAL PROBLEMS

Emotional problems are caused by the type of situational problems discussed in the previous section. Situational problems come from shock, changes, and stress. You can not help your emotionally disturbed relative or friend unless you can discover the *cause* of the emotional disturbance.

You may be able to find this out from the person himself. Some people are very much aware of the cause of their emotional problems. These people are frequently eager to discuss their problems. Other individuals, however, may not recognize the exact or true cause of their neurotic feelings or actions. There may be a subconscious desire not to admit to the situation that is causing the emotional reaction. There are also individuals who do know the causes but for reasons which may range from ignorance to guilt will not admit the connection. These individuals are usually reluctant to discuss their emotional problem.

The best way to discover the situational problem that is causing an emotional problem is to play the part of a detective. Try to reconstruct the events preceding the onset of neurotic behavior. Look for clues in what your family member or friend is doing or saying. Be *non-emotional* about this attempt to discover the situational problem. Don't blind yourself to the truth by preconceived ideas.

Knowledge of the situational problem is a forward step in helping the emotionally disturbed person to adjust to reality.

REASONS FOR NEUROTIC BEHAVIOR

We have been talking about *causes* and *symptoms* of neurotic behavior; there are also *reasons* for this behavior.

If we were to program the steps of neurotic behavior it would look like this:

1. Situational problem (Cause)
2. Reasons for reaction (Action)
3. Symptoms (Result)

There are five basic reasons for reaction to situational problems. These reasons vary according to the individual. They also vary according to the particular situation. Therefore, an individual may surprise us by responding in one way to one situation and in an entirely different way in another situation.

FIVE BASIC REASONS FOR REACTION

1. Ignorance
2. Embarrassment
3. Shame
4. Guilt
5. Fear

Young people and inexperienced people frequently have emotional problems because of ignorance. They become involved in an action which turns into a situational problem. They are unable to properly assess the importance of this problem. They are unable to understand it.

A high school girl became severely depressed. Her parents were at a loss to explain the sudden change in her personality. A counselor discovered that the girl, who had recently received permission to date, was so ignorant of sexual matters that she thought she would become pregnant if she permitted even the slightest degree of intimacy.

Embarrassment may cause the reaction to a stress situation. An individual may feel too embarrassed to discuss his problem or to seek help. Instead, he suffers in silence, and his neurotic symptoms appear.

Mona suddenly developed withdrawal symptoms, digestive disturbances, and irritability. Her friends could not understand her anti-social attitude. Her family was worried and concerned. Finally someone discovered that Mona had been publicly rebuked by her boss for an error. Although some persons would have reacted in anger, Mona felt only shame. That shame caused her to try to avoid a similar incident by *withdrawing*. Her subconscious wish was aided by physical symptoms. She thus could justify her anti-social actions by the excuse of not feeling well. The expected, natural irritation toward her boss had been transferred to a general attitude of irritability.

Mona was helped after she was able to talk over the scolding incident and put it in its proper perspective.

Guilt is also a common reaction. The person who assumes a false or unwarranted responsibility will often have guilty feelings. These feelings will be exhibited in neurotic behavior.

Eva, a widow, considered herself responsible for her family's welfare. It was actually impossible for Eva to do all the things that she thought were necessary. Eva felt guilty because she thought that she was failing in her duty. That sense of guilt caused her to adopt strange compulsive habits of behavior. She went through an elaborate ritual of locking the house each night. She would cook only in certain pans and use only certain foods. She became *obsessed* by cleanliness.

Eva finally sought help after a close friend convinced her that she had allowed emotional problems to overwhelm her. After treatment, Eva was able to be more realistic about her family situation. Instead of assuming all the responsibility herself, she made it a shared family experience. She learned to relax.

Fear as a reaction is also not unusual. This is often true in relation to physical health problems.

An individual has a physical symptom. He does not seek medical aid but reacts in fear. He imagines that this symptom is a sign of serious disease. The *fear* reaction causes him to develop neurotic habits of thought and behavior.

AMBIVALENCE AS A CAUSE OF EMOTIONAL PROBLEMS

Learning to help the person with emotional problems sometimes means changing your own attitude. This is especially important when the other person is involved in an emotionally close relationship with you.

Ambivalence, which is often difficult for people to understand and accept, is a common cause of *neurotic* behavior. Ambivalence is *contradictory* feelings or attitudes. These may be conscious or unconscious. Usually the individual is disturbed by his mixed love and hate feelings. Rather than acknowledge the existence of these feelings, he will try to camouflage them by some form of neurotic behavior.

It may be equally difficult for you to accept ambivalence if it is directed at you or at your relationship to the individual.

Ambivalence is not a sign of unnatural feeling. It is not a sign of indifference. It is not the end to a relationship.

The reasons for an ambivalent attitude, just like the reasons for any other emotional problem, must be discovered and treated.

Recently a young mother came to me in tears. She had begun to have violent outbursts of temper. She was afraid that she might hurt her new baby.

A discussion of her problem revealed that she had *ambivalent feelings* toward the baby. She loved him, but she also hated him because she felt tied down by her new duties of motherhood. She was actually more frightened than angry.

"Do you think I'm crazy?" she asked.

This question is frequently asked by patients who fear the worst when actually their emotional troubles are not that complicated or severe.

Assured that her problem was not unusual and that she was not

a "bad" mother, she was able to be more rational about her problem. Since one of her difficulties was not being able to cope with the physical details of caring for an infant, it was arranged that she be given instruction. It was also recommended that she leave the baby at least one afternoon a week with a competent person while she did something not related to her position as "a mother."

I have seen cases of neurosis where the emotional problem has been caused by feelings of ambivalence toward aged parents. It can also happen when a marriage partner becomes ill or disabled.

Why Mrs. H. Suffered from Chronic Fatigue

Mr. and Mrs. H. had been married for 25 years but now their marriage was in jeopardy. The reason—Mrs. H's *chronic fatigue.*

Suddenly her behavior had changed. Her attitude toward her marriage, toward her home, and toward her husband had changed. Formerly an efficient housekeeper and a good cook, Mrs. H. now could not find the energy to keep the house in order. She either served frozen dinners, or they ate out.

Their social life suffered, for Mrs. H. was too exhausted to take part in social activities. She had become forgetful and irritable as well. It was no wonder that Mr. H. was unhappy with his marital situation!

The cause of Mrs. H's sudden neurotic behavior was her guilt over placing her aged father in a nursing home. Somehow in her emotional thinking she had come to the illogical and wrong conclusion that because she had done this, she was no good. She lost her self-esteem and all interest in her surroundings.

Once Mrs. H. was able to face her feelings in a sensible, non-emotional way, she was on the road to recovery. It took outside aid, though, to convince her that society was *not* going to blame her for putting her father in a home. It took time to convince her that she had done the *best* thing from a practical point of view.

In time, Mrs. H. was able to admit these facts. She could see that there was not room for her father in the H. home. She could see that her father actually got *better* care and was *more* comfortable in the nursing home.

Most important of all, Mrs. H. finally realized that her *first* duty was toward her husband and her home.

HOW TO DISTINGUISH BETWEEN NEUROSIS AND PSYCHOSIS

Neurosis and *psychosis* are not the same. A neurotic is an *emotionally* disturbed person. A psychotic is *mentally* disturbed.

A neurotic, while suffering emotionally, is usually still able to function in most life areas. He is ill but not totally incapacitated.

A psychotic is seriously ill and requires hospitalization and psychiatric care. He is usually disoriented and out of touch with reality.

A neurotic might become overly concerned about health problems. He makes a nuisance of himself by talking about this, by insisting that his friends should adopt certain health habits and eat only certain foods. For example, a woman I know gives out booklets on a special health diet to all her acquaintances. Neurotic—yes, but harmless.

A psychotic might also become concerned about health problems. In his case, however, it has more serious consequences. He may have delusions about his status and think he is a doctor. He may want to actually prescribe treatment for other people. One patient had worked out an elaborate food plan that he claimed would prolong life. The difficulty was that he was suffering from malnutrition. When he refused to eat, he had to be force-fed.

Fortunately for the neurotics, they are curable by rational thought and advice. Time is also an aid, for the situational problems that cause emotional problems are often temporary. It is usually possible to make environmental and situational changes.

HOW YOU CAN RECEIVE OUTSIDE HELP FOR THE FAMILY MEMBER WITH EMOTIONAL PROBLEMS

It is often advisable to seek outside help in dealing with family emotional problems. You may be too close to the family member who needs help to give him what he needs. You may be too emotionally involved.

Although you can not *directly* help your emotionally ill family member, you can help by encouraging him to seek outside help. You can help by supporting the idea of getting help. You can help by being co-operative during the period of treatment.

The kind of outside help will depend upon the nature of the problem, the needs of the individual and the help that is readily available.

Some individuals need only a short period in which they can talk over their feelings with a third party. Others, however, need drug therapy or some form of treatment. While a single visit may clear up one neurotic's problem, another neurotic might require several visits. Psychoanalysis may be needed in some cases.

The objective third party can be the family physician, a lay counselor, a medical specialist such as a psychiatrist, or a minister.

If you are not sure where to go for help, ask your family doctor or your minister. They will not only be familiar with your family, but they are also aware of the community resources for dealing with emotional problems.

HOW TO RESPOND TOWARD THE NEUROTIC

Your response toward the neurotic can help to ease the situation. It is not easy to live with a neurotic. It is not always pleasant. It is at times a tense situation. There may even be periods of outright hostility. But, with patience and understanding, harmony and happiness can be restored to the household.

The most important thing to do is to refuse to be blamed or to blame yourself for the emotional problems of your family member. Recognizing that a neurosis is present does not mean accepting the responsibility for it.

The neurotic has to face reality. You can not do it for him. He has to accept reasonable solutions for himself. You can not provide solutions and *force* them on him.

You need to keep a kind of emotional moat between you and the neurotic. While maintaining attitudes of love, affection, and understanding, you must avoid letting yourself be used as a scapegoat.

"I used to get upset when my wife accused me of being a poor provider and unkind. I would often become angry, but then I realized that this was not true. She was emotionally ill and felt the need to reject me," Mr. F. said.

Fortunately, Mr. F. was able to keep his own emotions under control.

"I stopped taking her accusations personally," he went on to explain. "Sure enough, when she went for treatment, it came out that she was actually still angry with her *father* because he had been such a poor provider. A psychological counselor helped her discover this and she was later able to talk it over with me too."

It is best to avoid becoming part of the neurotic situation. You may have to remind yourself and the other person that you did not *create* the problem nor can you *solve* it.

HOW THE PAST INFLUENCES THE PRESENT

The neurosis of today is often an old unresolved emotional conflict from yesterday. It is as if you had a canvas on which a new picture is painted over an old one. The old picture is still there. Sometimes it is seen where the new paint is thinly or poorly applied. At other times, it needs a device like a special light to show up the hidden picture.

In emotional problems, the two pictures are also there. It sometimes takes analysis to bring out the one from the past. This was true with Mrs. F. who was blaming her husband for what were actually the misdeeds of her father.

The neurotic husband who insists that his wife does not love him enough is still complaining about the lack of love and affection he received from his mother. This may take the form of criticizing his wife's cooking, clothing and hair styles, or her opinions. He is, however, really criticizing his mother.

This is the process of *transference* which we have discussed in previous chapters. Transference of childhood attitudes to adult figures is usually focused upon the individual with whom the neurotic is most closely involved.

It is important that you realize the significance of this transference phenomenon and do not take it as a personal attack.

HOW THE CREATION OF THE RIGHT ATMOSPHERE AND ATTITUDE WILL HELP THE NEUROTIC OVERCOME EMOTIONAL ILLNESS

Once you have encouraged the neurotic to seek outside help, you have taken the first step in helping him to overcome his emotional illness. But, you can also do much to help him in this difficult period by creating the right atmosphere. You can help by having the right attitude.

The normal home atmosphere should be preserved. This should be an atmosphere of gentleness, love, and understanding. Despite what might seem like provocation, the home should not be a center for scoldings, recriminations or hurt feelings.

Your total aim should be to assist the neurotic by keeping a calm attitude. *Tension can be catching.* Try to avoid adding to the stress of the emotionally ill person.

HOW FAMILY LIFE CAN BE PRESERVED IN HARMONY DURING TIMES OF EMOTIONAL PROBLEMS

Any type of crisis has its effect on family life. This can be an emotional illness, physical illness, or any sudden loss.

Physical illness is more easily understood and accepted by family members. They can see its effects. They can see its cure.

Emotional illness is more difficult to accept. It is not always as visible. It is rarely predictable and the cure is not always when anticipated. In its course, it is often a seesaw illness. It is a very personal illness and can not be understood by some individuals.

"I could understand the pain my wife had when she broke her leg," Clark S. said, "but I don't understand those neck pains she has now. She says they are excruciating pains and are keeping her from enjoying life. The doctor says they are caused by tension. I don't know why she should be tense; she has everything she need or wants!"

Obviously some work had to be done with Clark so that family harmony could be restored. His wife's tension was caused by emotional reasons. Her husband's attitude only added to her tension.

Eventually Clark learned to show his wife the same kindness

and consideration during her period of *emotional* illness as he had shown her during her physical illness.

Normal family life routines should continue as much as possible during periods of emotional stress. In fact, many neurotics welcome these routines and cling to them as safety lifelines.

"I always knew that my family was pulling for me to get better. They all did their best to see that I never felt like a bother to them. Although I am sure that there were times that my emotional outbursts must have caused them distress, they did not show it to me," said a former patient, adding, "It was their kindness and understanding that made it possible for me to solve my problems as quickly as I did."

Can the emotionally upset member of *your* family say that about *his* family?

CHECK LIST FOR HELPING THE NEUROTIC AT HOME

This check list is a ten-point list of the practical things you should be doing to help the neurotic at home. These same things will also help *you* and other members of the family to live with the neurotic and his emotional problems.
Ask yourself:

1. Have you encouraged or assisted him to find help?
2. Have you tried to understand the nature of his particular problem?
3. Are you willing to listen to him when he wants to talk?
4. Are you able to avoid feelings of anger, pity, irritation or contempt for him?
5. Do you see that he has relaxation, rest, and the proper diet?
6. Do you understand the meaning of *transference?*
7. Can you continue to display kindness, affection, and gentleness in the face of hostility, irritation, or seemingly illogical attitudes?
8. Are you doing your best to keep family life and traditions intact?
9. Are you patient with him?
10. Do you have a *positive* attitude toward him and his future?

You may want to use this as a reminder list.

No, it is *not* easy to live with a person who has emotional problems, but it does not need to become a domestic disaster.

You are part of the treatment process. You can help him back to good emotional health.

A REMINDER

It is not a disgrace to have an emotional problem or neurosis. It is not a reflection on the family.

Since people respond in *different* ways to stress and to situational problems, it is not possible to predict *exact* reactions.

Outside help should be sought for the family member who has an emotional problem. The family can do its part by having *positive* attitudes toward the neurotic. Family life can continue without disruption.

Neurotic behavior is not unusual. It is often temporary. It is not the same as psychotic behavior. *It can be helped.*

INDEX

Accidents and illness, how to cope with, 177-192
accident-prone child or adult, handling, 182-183
anger as cause, 177-178
bona fide accidents and illnesses, accepting, 187-188
in family circle, adjusting to, 188-189
illness, regression in, 189
inferiority, feelings of, 178-179
as opportunity for more learning and maturation, 191
parent image and adult behavior in, 183
personality, accident-prone, how to change, 186-187
psychosomatic illnesses, understanding, 187
self-punishment motivations, 179-182
discovering, 181-182
and sex, 183-184
test to determine accident-proneness, 184-186
your own, coping with, 189-191
Accidents caused by work, 88-89
Advancement in work, preparing for, 93-94
Aggression as immature attitude toward leisure, 99
Alone in modern society, 193-194
Altruism as cure for loneliness, 207-208
Ambivalence as cause for emotional problems, 215-217
Anesthesia as psychosomatic illness, 49
Anger as cause of accidents, 177-178
Anxiety, feelings of as sign of impending emotional problem, 37, 38
Anxiety state in work situation, how to detect, 82
Appetite, loss of as symptom of impending emotional problems, 43
Aptitude as good reason for work choice, 91
Aptitude-interest test to determine natural aptitudes, 92
Artistic interests as good use of leisure time, 106

Asthma of psychosomatic origin, 48
Attitudes toward leisure, immature, six, 99-100

Bickering as expression of family conflict, 164
Blunt criticism, 110
Bonaparte, Princess Marie, 144
Breathing difficulties as symptom of psychosomatic illness, 48

"C's," three big, as needs in marriage, 151-152
Capacity, work, finding level of, 92
Carlyle, Thomas, 82
Chain reaction criticism, how to handle, 117-118
Challenges in life, learning to accept for new self-image, 65
Chance as lazy method of job selection, 91
Changing choice of work, 91-92
Checklist, personal, for happiness, 33-35
Childhood frustrations, reflection of in adult use of leisure time, 98-99
Childhood mental injuries and happiness, 28-29
Childhood training and traumas, effect of on family attitudes, 166-167
Childhood trauma and adult sex problems, 140-142
Children, handling loneliness in, 204-206
"Chip on the shoulder" as evidence of mental block, 70-71
Choice of certain work, reasons for, 89-92
changing, 91-92
Ten-Point Work Choice Scale, 89-91
Choosing self you want to be, 64
Choosing special interest for use of leisure time, 107
Churchill, Sir Winston, 112
Civic interests as good use of leisure time, 107

223